Money Skills for Teens and Young Adults: Interactive Challenges to Take Control and Pay Your Own Way

Balance Wants vs. Needs, Build Smart Money Habits, and Spend Confidently Without the Fear of Going Broke

BY ROSE LYONS

Contents

Introduction:
Why Save?

Welcome **to your ultimate guide to saving mone**y—but let's be real, this isn't just another finance book. This is about *you*—the choices you make today, the actions you take, and the rewards waiting for you down the road. Every dollar you put away brings you closer to unlocking your dreams, whether that's snagging the latest game, treating your best friend to something special, or even setting yourself up for bigger goals like a car or epic future adventures.

Saving money isn't about missing out—it's about making sure you can say "yes" to the things you love when the time comes. This book is here to show you how saving is not just about numbers—it's about *you* taking control of your money, your future, and your freedom. You're not just learning how to stash cash; you're building skills that will help you dominate life—like patience, discipline, and learning how to get what you want without stress.

The best part? Saving doesn't have to be boring or feel like a sacrifice. It's all about how you approach it—turning it into a game where the winner is *you*. This book is packed with fun, realistic challenges that'll help you save for what matters most, without feeling like you're giving anything up.

Before we dive in, take a moment to talk to your parents or guardians about how they learned to manage money. Ask them:

> **How were they taught about wants vs. needs?**
>
> **What was important for them to save for when they were your age?**
>
> **If no one taught them, when did they start learning how to save?**
>
> **What kinds of things did they struggle with by not being taught this information?**

These conversations will help you understand that you're not alone in figuring all of this out—everyone has their own learning curve. You might even learn about the challenges your parents faced because they didn't have a guide like this when they were younger.

So, let's get started. It's time to flip the script on what saving really means and start taking action. With every smart choice you make, you're not just saving money—you're building the life *you* want. And trust me, the rewards are totally worth it!

How to Use This Book

This book is your roadmap and toolkit for mastering the art of saving. Each chapter introduces a new aspect of saving, with challenges that grow more complex as you build confidence in your skills. Here's how to get the most out of it:

> **Start Simple:** Begin with the basics and ease into the more advanced challenges. There's no rush—saving is a marathon, not a sprint.
>
> **Track Your Progress:** Use the templates and trackers included to keep an eye on your achievements. Seeing your progress in real-time is a huge motivator, and it helps you stay on track.
>
> **Reflect:** After each challenge, take a moment to reflect on your experience. What did you learn? What worked, and what could you improve next time? Reflection is key to growing your skills.

Celebrate: Don't forget to celebrate your milestones, no matter how small. Each achievement is progress toward your larger goal of financial independence. Rewarding yourself along the way keeps things fun and engaging.

Get Involved: Talk to your family and friends about what you're learning. Sharing your progress and challenges makes the journey more enjoyable and can inspire those around you.

Are you ready to take the first step towards mastering your money? Let's dive in! Remember, this journey is about *progress, not perfection*. Here's to achieving your dreams, one savings challenge at a time!

Chapter 1:

Understanding Money

Money: What Is It, Really?

At its core, money is a tool that humans have used throughout history to trade goods and services. Long before the dollars and cents we use today, people traded items directly in a system known as bartering. Imagine trading a basket of apples for a wool blanket or even a video game with friends! As societies grew more complex, so did their needs, leading to the creation of money as a universal medium of exchange.

Money has three main functions:

Medium of Exchange: It allows us to buy and sell goods and services (like buying lunch or a new game).

Unit of Account: It provides a way to measure the value of something (like comparing the cost of different sneakers).

Store of Value: It can be saved and used in the future, retaining its value over time (like saving for a concert).

Earning Money

Earning money is the first big step in your financial journey. For many teens, this might start with small, manageable tasks like getting an allowance for completing chores around the house, babysitting for a neighbor, or helping out with tutoring. These early experiences with earning money help you understand the value of hard work and responsibility. But as you grow, you might explore other ways to earn, like picking up local community jobs or even finding gigs online. Whether it's walking dogs, mowing lawns, or selling your skills in graphic design or social media management, the opportunities are out there, and the money you earn is all yours.

What makes earning money so empowering is the freedom and independence it gives you. You're not relying on anyone else to fund your goals or cover your expenses—it's your effort and determination that translate directly into financial rewards. Imagine being able to buy those concert tickets you've been eyeing, save up for new gaming equipment, or even start building up a fund for your first car, all with the money you earned yourself. It's a powerful feeling when your hard work pays off, and you're able to make decisions about how you spend, save, and invest.

Not only does earning your own money feel rewarding, but it also teaches you important life skills that will help you in the future. By earning, you're learning about budgeting, prioritizing your needs and wants, and understanding the effort it takes to build financial security. You'll start to see that every dollar has potential—whether it goes toward something fun or toward building up savings for something bigger down the road. And when you do reach those goals, whether it's buying something you've been saving for or simply having a financial cushion, you'll feel proud knowing that you achieved it through your own hard work.

Spending Wisely

Spending is where things get interesting (and sometimes tricky). Spending wisely means understanding the difference between wants and needs, but it doesn't mean you have to give up on the things you want altogether. It's about knowing when to prioritize needs and how to plan for your wants through smart saving.

> **Needs:** Essentials like food, clothing, shelter, transportation, and healthcare. These are non-negotiable, meaning you need them to get through your day-to-day life.
>
> **Wants:** These are things that enhance your lifestyle but aren't essential for survival, like the latest smartphone, designer sneakers, or tickets to a concert.

One of the most important aspects of spending wisely is learning to sacrifice some of your wants in the short term to make sure your needs are met. But that doesn't mean you'll never get what you want. This is where **savings goals** come into play. By setting aside money for your wants, you can still enjoy the things you love—without putting your needs or financial security at risk.

Balancing Wants and Needs with a Budget

A key part of responsible spending is creating a budget. A budget helps you plan how to allocate your money to cover your needs first and then save up for your wants. Think of it as a game plan: you're deciding how much goes to essentials, how much can be saved, and how much you can use for fun. Budgeting helps you stay focused on your financial goals while avoiding the temptation to spend impulsively on wants.

Sacrificing Wants Today, Enjoying Them Tomorrow

Sacrificing a want today doesn't mean you're giving it up forever. In fact, having a plan and a savings goal makes getting what you want even more rewarding because you've worked for it and can afford it guilt-free. For example, you might decide to skip eating out a few times so you can save for a new video game or pair of sneakers.

Money Skills for Teens and Young Adults

By saving specifically for what you want, you get to enjoy the reward without risking your ability to cover your needs.

The Power of Savings Goals

Setting clear savings goals gives you control over your financial decisions. When you have a goal in mind—like saving for a concert, a new gadget, or a vacation—it becomes easier to put money aside, even if it means delaying gratification. You'll be able to look forward to getting what you want, knowing that you've done it responsibly. Plus, when you reach that goal, it feels a lot more satisfying than spending impulsively and dealing with financial stress later.

A Simple Wants vs. Needs Chart

Here's a simple way to break down your spending categories:

The Balance

Spending wisely doesn't mean eliminating all your wants—it means finding a balance. By prioritizing your needs and setting savings goals for your wants, you'll be able to enjoy both. The key is making sure you're not sacrificing your financial stability to satisfy short-term desires. With discipline, patience, and smart saving, you can meet your needs and still get what you want in a way that makes sense for your future.

Needs	Food, Rent, Utilities, Basic Clothing, Transportation	High Priority—These come first
Wants	New Video Game, Concert Tickets, Designer Shoes, Dining Out	Lower Priority—These can wait or be saved for.

The Art of Saving

Saving Money: A Long-Term Strategy

Saving money is about setting aside a portion of what you earn for future use rather than spending it immediately. It teaches you to think ahead, preparing not only for things you know are coming—like buying a new game, a car, or saving for college—but also for unexpected events, like emergencies. Saving builds patience, discipline, and the ability to think long-term. Every dollar you set aside brings you closer to your goal, and reaching those goals becomes incredibly rewarding because you worked for it step by step. Plus, when life throws a curveball, you'll have the peace of mind knowing you're prepared.

Track Your Spending and Save Smarter

One of the best ways to take control of your finances is by tracking your spending. For at least two weeks, write down every single penny you spend—whether it's on a snack, a new game, or something small like coffee. This might feel tedious, but it's eye-opening and shows where your money actually goes. You can use apps like YNAB (You Need a Budget), or simply jot it down in a notebook. Once you have this record, take a close look at it. You'll probably notice how much you're spending on non-essential items. Now's the time to make adjustments. Try cutting discretionary spending by 50%. For example, if you're spending $20 a week on coffee, aim to cut it down to $10. This small change—like making coffee at home—can save you more money than you realize, and the extra cash can go straight toward your savings goals.

Create a Budget for What You Love

Saving money doesn't mean cutting out everything you enjoy. In fact, budgeting is all about making sure you can still enjoy the things you love—responsibly. Set a monthly budget for activities like going out to eat, shopping, or entertainment. By setting limits, you can indulge in your favorite treats without overspending. The money you save from cutting back on non-essentials can be redirected toward your

savings goals, like saving for a car or a special purchase. Budgeting lets you enjoy your favorite things guilt-free because you've planned for them while still making progress toward your larger financial goals.

Empower Yourself Through Saving and Budgeting

Tracking your spending and setting a budget isn't about restricting yourself—it's about empowerment. When you know where your money is going and make intentional choices about cutting back on unnecessary expenses, you're taking control of your future. The money you save can be used for bigger goals like a vacation, a new gadget, or even a safety net for emergencies. Start today by tracking your spending, creating a budget, and challenging yourself to save. You'll be surprised how much power you feel when your financial goals become more attainable with each step.

Why Saving and Budgeting Are So Important

Saving money isn't just about building wealth; it's about securing your future and being prepared for both opportunities and challenges. Budgeting allows you to make informed decisions about where your money goes, ensuring that your spending aligns with your goals. Developing good saving and budgeting habits now will create a strong financial foundation that will benefit you throughout your life. Whether you're saving for something fun, like a concert, or something essential, like an emergency fund, these habits will give you the freedom and peace of mind that come with financial security.

Starting Your Saving and Budgeting Journey

Now that you understand the basics of earning, spending, and saving, it's time to put these skills into action. Start by setting a small, achievable savings goal—like saving for concert tickets or a new gadget. This goal will motivate you as you practice tracking your income and expenses. Create a budget to allocate a portion of your earnings toward your goal. As you see progress, you'll feel empowered to continue saving and managing your finances wisely. Remember, even the smallest steps toward saving

and budgeting can lead to significant financial gains over time. Start today, and see where your money management journey takes you!

Final Thoughts: Empower Yourself Through Saving and Budgeting

Saving and budgeting are powerful tools that put you in control of your financial future. By tracking your spending, creating a budget, and setting clear savings goals, you'll make real progress toward achieving your dreams. Whether it's something small now or a bigger goal later, the steps you take today will make a huge difference. You've got the tools—now make that first step count. You'll be amazed at how far you can go.

PURCHASES
Tracker

Date	Price	Store	Item	Want	Need

Chapter 2:
Setting Your First Savings Goal

The Power of Goal-Setting

Welcome to the next step in your financial journey—setting your first savings goal. Why is goal-setting so important? Think of it like entering a destination into a navigation app. Without a specific destination, you're just driving around with no clear direction, and it's easy to get lost or distracted. When you set a savings goal, you're giving yourself a clear target to aim for, which keeps you focused and motivated. It turns the vague idea of "I should save money" into something specific and actionable. You'll know exactly what you're working toward and can measure your progress along the way, which makes the whole process feel more rewarding.

For example, if your goal is to save $500 for a new laptop, that's a lot easier to work toward than just vaguely thinking, "I need to save some money." Having a concrete

goal in place helps you make better decisions, like skipping an impulse purchase because you know it will slow down your progress. Each time you save a little more, you're one step closer to achieving something you really want, and that feeling of progress can keep you motivated to stay on track.

Understanding Your Motivation

Before you can set your goal, it's important to understand *why* you want to save money in the first place. This motivation is your personal "why" and it's what will keep you going when saving feels tough or when distractions come up. Ask yourself: *What's my reason for saving?* It might be something short-term, like buying a new video game, upgrading your phone, or going to a concert. Or maybe you have a bigger goal in mind, like saving for a car, starting a college fund or even traveling abroad after high school. Some people are motivated by the peace of mind that comes from building an emergency fund, so they know they're prepared for the unexpected.

Whatever your motivation, make sure it's something that really matters to you. If you're passionate about what you're saving for, you're more likely to stay committed, even when it means making small sacrifices along the way. Once you know what you're working toward, you can break it down into smaller, more manageable steps, like saving a certain amount each week or month. This makes the whole process less overwhelming and keeps you focused on the end goal. Whether your goal is big or small, understanding why you're saving gives your plan purpose and keeps you motivated, no matter how long it takes to reach that goal.

Activity: Define Your Goal

Let's make it official. Grab a pen and use the section below, or open a notes app on your device, and follow these steps:

Name Your Savings

Give your goal a catchy name to make it more personal and exciting. Instead of just "concert savings," how about calling it the "Front Row Dream Fund"?

This not only makes it sound more fun but also reminds you exactly why you're saving—so you can rock out with your favorite band without worrying about money.

What to Save For

Write down exactly what you're saving for. Be as specific as possible. Instead of just writing "for a concert," include details like "tickets to see my favorite band's summer tour" or "VIP passes for the front row at the fall music festival." Being specific makes the goal feel more real and exciting.

Why are you saving?

Explain why this concert is important to you. Maybe it's your favorite artist's first tour, or it's an experience you've been dreaming of with friends. Knowing why you're saving will help you stay motivated and focused on your goal when temptations arise.

How Much You Need

Research the total cost of attending the concert, including tickets, transportation, and even a little extra for merch. Write down the full amount you need to save. Breaking it down like this turns your dream of going to the concert into a measurable, achievable target.

Deadline

Set a realistic deadline for when you want to buy your tickets. Do you need the money before they go on sale, or is the concert a few months away? Having a clear timeframe helps you break your savings goal into smaller, manageable steps, like saving a certain amount each week.

NAME OF YOUR GOAL

IMPORTANT!

....

SAVINGS GOAL

| WHAT ARE YOU SAVING FOR? | ◆ .... ◆
 ◆ .... ◆
 ◆ .... ◆ |

| WHY IS IT IMPORTANT TO YOU? | ◆ .... ◆
 ◆ .... ◆
 ◆ .... ◆ |

| DUE BY? | ◆ .... ◆ |

Breaking It Down: The Savings Plan

With your goal defined, it's time to break it down into a plan that feels doable. If your goal seems overwhelming at first, remember that every big achievement starts with small, manageable steps. By taking it one piece at a time, you'll stay on track and make steady progress toward that concert experience you've been dreaming about.

Monthly Savings Target

Start by dividing the total amount you need by the number of months you have until your deadline. For example, if you need $200 and the concert is in five months, divide $200 by 5 months, which gives you a target of $40 per month. This helps turn a big, scary number into a more manageable goal.

Is that $40/month realistic with your current allowance or income? If it seems too high, don't worry—this is where you can adjust. You have two options: either extend your deadline to give yourself more time to save or find ways to boost your income, like picking up an extra chore, babysitting, or selling something you no longer need. The key is to stay flexible while keeping your goal in sight.

Weekly Check-ins

Once you've figured out your monthly savings target, break it down further by dividing it by four to get a weekly savings goal. In the same example, $40 per month becomes just $10 a week. This makes your goal feel even more achievable—because setting aside $10 each week sounds a lot easier than thinking about saving $200 all at once.

Doing weekly check-ins keeps you accountable and helps you track your progress. Every week, take a moment to see how much you've saved and how much further you have to go. If you're falling behind, you can adjust your plan—maybe cut back on a small treat or look for other ways to earn a little extra. On the flip side, if you're ahead of schedule, give yourself a pat on the back and keep that momentum going!

Stay Flexible

If life happens and you need to spend some of your savings on an unexpected expense, don't be discouraged. Adjust your plan and keep going. The key to reaching your goal is consistency, not perfection.

By breaking your goal into monthly and weekly steps, you'll make steady progress without feeling overwhelmed. Each small step gets you closer to that front-row concert experience!

MONTHLY SAVINGS TARGET

- How many months to due date? ....
- Divide Savings Goal by # of months ....

Just remember "slow & steady wins the race"

Weekly Check-ins

Color the money bag with colors that indicate status

- Blue – Above the Target
- Green – Same as Target
- Red – Less than Target

Month [ ]

WEEK [ ] — AMT SAVED [ ]
WEEK [ ] — AMT SAVED [ ]
WEEK [ ] — AMT SAVED [ ]
WEEK [ ] — AMT SAVED [ ]
TOTAL SAVED [ ]

Month [ ]

WEEK [ ] — AMT SAVED [ ]
WEEK [ ] — AMT SAVED [ ]
WEEK [ ] — AMT SAVED [ ]
WEEK [ ] — AMT SAVED [ ]
TOTAL SAVED [ ]

Month [ ]

WEEK [ ] — AMT SAVED [ ]
WEEK [ ] — AMT SAVED [ ]
WEEK [ ] — AMT SAVED [ ]
WEEK [ ] — AMT SAVED [ ]
TOTAL SAVED [ ]

Month [ ]

WEEK [ ] — AMT SAVED [ ]
WEEK [ ] — AMT SAVED [ ]
WEEK [ ] — AMT SAVED [ ]
WEEK [ ] — AMT SAVED [ ]
TOTAL SAVED [ ]

Month [ ]

WEEK [ ] — AMT SAVED [ ]
WEEK [ ] — AMT SAVED [ ]
WEEK [ ] — AMT SAVED [ ]
WEEK [ ] — AMT SAVED [ ]
TOTAL SAVED [ ]

The Importance of Flexibility

Your first savings goal is a great introduction to financial planning, but it's important to remember that life doesn't always go as planned. Unexpected expenses, like car repairs, a decrease in income, or even a spontaneous opportunity, can come up and throw off your original savings plan—and that's perfectly okay. The key is to stay flexible and not get discouraged when things change.

Adjusting your savings goal isn't a sign of failure; it's actually a sign of smart financial management. Life will always have surprises, and part of being financially responsible is knowing how to adapt when those surprises pop up. Maybe you need to put some of your savings towards something urgent or delay reaching your goal a little longer. By remaining flexible and adjusting your plan when necessary, you're showing that you can manage both the expected and the unexpected.

Being adaptable with your savings goals now prepares you for bigger financial decisions later. Whether it's dealing with an emergency, taking advantage of a sudden opportunity, or simply recalculating your timeline, learning to pivot without giving up will set you up for success in the long run. Flexibility isn't a setback—it's how you stay in control of your financial future, no matter what comes your way.

Visualize Your Goal

Creating a visual representation of your savings goal is a great way to stay motivated and engaged in the process. When you can actually see how far you've come and how close you are to reaching your goal, it gives you a sense of accomplishment and keeps you focused. There are plenty of creative ways to make this happen.

One simple option is to draw a progress bar on a poster or a whiteboard. Divide the bar into sections that represent different milestones in your savings goal. As you save, fill in each section to visually track how much closer you're getting. It's a tangible reminder of your progress that you can update regularly, making the process more interactive.

You could also use a savings app to track your progress digitally. Many apps allow you to set a target amount and visually track how close you are to reaching it. Plus, they often come with helpful features like reminders to save or alerts when you hit milestones, keeping you accountable.

Another fun approach is to craft a physical savings jar. Label the jar with your goal, whether it's $100 for a new gadget or $500 for a bigger purchase. Each time you add money to the jar, you'll literally see it fill up, making the savings journey more rewarding. You can even decorate the jar with stickers or quotes that inspire you to keep going.

The idea behind these visual tools is to make your goal feel more real and immediate. Instead of your savings just being an abstract number in a bank account, it becomes something you interact with regularly. It's easier to stay motivated when you can see exactly how your efforts are paying off. Every bit you save, no matter how small, feels like progress when you can watch your savings grow in front of you.

Savings JAR

Color the jar every time you achieve a milestone..
Let's Get Started !!!

Saving for: ....

Goal: $ ....

Learn how to calculate %

$$\% \text{ savings} = \frac{\text{current savings}}{\text{final savings}} \times 100$$

For Example,

current savings : $ 150
Final Savings : $500

$$\% \text{ savings} = \frac{150}{500} \times 100$$

$$= 0.3 \times 100$$

$$= 30\%$$

Congrats!!
You turned your dreams into reality!

- 100 % of your savings goal achieved

  🎖 Completed on ....

- 90 % of your savings goal achieved

- 80 % of your savings goal achieved

- 70 % of your savings goal achieved

- 60 % of your savings goal achieved

- 50 % of your savings goal achieved

- 40 % of your savings goal achieved

- 30 % of your savings goal achieved

- 20 % of your savings goal achieved

- 10 % of your savings goal achieved

- 5 % of your savings goal achieved

- First savings

Sharing Your Goal: The Role of Accountability

One of the best ways to stay motivated while saving is to share your goal with someone you trust, whether it's a close friend, a family member, or even a mentor. Sharing your goal makes it feel more concrete, like you're really committing to it, and it adds a layer of accountability. When someone else knows about your plan, it's easier to stay on track because you've essentially told someone, "I'm going to do this." That external accountability can give you an extra push to keep saving, even on days when you might feel like spending.

Plus, the person you share your goal with might offer more than just encouragement. They could give you advice, share their own experience with saving, or even join you in setting their own savings goal. Having someone to talk to about your progress, challenges, and wins makes the whole process more engaging and enjoyable. You're no longer going through it alone—you have a support system to cheer you on and keep you accountable. This social aspect can make a big difference when it comes to sticking with your goal over time.

Celebrate Milestones

It's important to celebrate the progress you make along the way, not just when you reach the final goal. Setting mini-milestones helps you stay motivated because you're not waiting for one big payoff at the end—you get to enjoy smaller victories along the way. For example, if your goal is to save $200, set milestones at $50, $100, and $150. Each time you hit one of these smaller targets, give yourself permission to celebrate. This could be as simple as treating yourself to something small you enjoy, like a favorite snack, or asking your parents to fund a small reward for your hard work.

Celebrating milestones doesn't just make saving more fun—it also helps you acknowledge the effort you've put in and keeps your motivation high. When you recognize the progress you've made, it boosts your confidence and reminds you that you're capable of reaching the final goal. Plus, breaking your goal into smaller chunks makes the process feel more manageable, so you're less likely to get discouraged.

Money Skills for Teens and Young Adults

Reflect and Learn

As you work towards your savings goal, it's helpful to reflect on your progress and the journey you've taken so far. Ask yourself: *What challenges did I face? How did I overcome them? Did I learn anything new about my spending habits or how I manage money?* Reflection is a powerful tool for personal growth, and it helps you become more financially savvy with each goal you set.

Taking the time to reflect also allows you to appreciate how much you've learned about budgeting and saving. You may notice areas where you've become more disciplined or patterns in your spending that you weren't aware of before. This reflection can guide you in setting future savings goals and help you adjust your approach as needed. The more you learn about yourself and your financial habits, the better equipped you'll be to reach bigger and more complex goals in the future.

 # Reflect & Learn

What Challenges did you face?

....

....

....

How did you overcome them?

....

....

....

What did you a learn about your spending habits?

....

....

....

How can you continue to improve?

....

....

....

Your First Goal: Just the Beginning

Reaching your first savings goal is a huge accomplishment, but it's really just the start of something much bigger. Think of this as the foundation for your entire financial journey. With every goal you set and achieve, whether it's saving for a new video game or working towards something larger like a car or a trip, you're not just collecting money—you're building confidence, developing new skills, and learning more about how to manage your finances. Each success shows you what you're capable of and gives you the motivation to keep going.

This process of setting goals, sticking to a plan, and seeing the results will serve you for a lifetime. The small, everyday decisions you're making now—choosing to save instead of spend—are creating habits that will help you manage bigger financial responsibilities later. Imagine how much more prepared you'll feel for challenges like paying for college, buying a house, or even starting your own business someday because you started honing these skills early on. Each goal you meet is a stepping stone toward a future where you're in control of your financial life.

Don't be afraid to dream big, but remember that it's okay to start small. Even the most ambitious goals begin with simple steps. Maybe your next savings target will be a little bigger, or maybe you'll take what you've learned and apply it to new areas of your life—like creating a budget for your first job or setting up an emergency fund. The important thing is that you keep moving forward. The more you practice, the better you'll get, and the more prepared you'll be for whatever comes your way.

Embrace the journey, knowing that the skills you're developing now will benefit your future self in ways you can't even imagine yet. Financial independence, security, and the ability to make choices without worrying about money—these are the rewards waiting for you as you continue on this path. So, keep dreaming big, setting goals, and embracing the lessons along the way. Your future self will look back and be so grateful that you started now.

Chapter 3:
Your First
Savings Challenge

Setting your first savings goal is a big step! Now, it's time to start your savings journey with some fun and rewarding challenges. These activities are designed to not only help you stay on track but also build strong financial habits that will set you up for success—both now and in the future. By diving into these challenges, you'll learn how to manage your money wisely while still enjoying the things you love.

Challenge 1: The Smart Saver Week

This challenge is all about flexing your willpower and resisting those tempting impulse buys for a whole week. That means saying "no" to those snacks, apps, and online shopping splurges you don't really need, and instead, saving that cash. Every time you skip an impulse purchase, add that money to your savings stash and watch it grow.

Set a Visible Goal

Write down your savings goal for the week and put it somewhere you can see every day. Whether it's on your phone, your bathroom mirror, or your desk, having that goal in sight will remind you why you're making these small sacrifices. It's like having a mini scoreboard to track your progress.

Reflection Time

At the end of the week, take a few minutes to reflect on how things went. How many times did you almost give in to buying something on a whim? More importantly, how awesome did it feel to watch your savings grow instead? Reflection helps you see how small choices add up, giving you the motivation to keep going.

Each week, as you tackle new challenges, you'll get stronger in your ability to save and manage your money. Remember, this isn't just about this one week—it's about creating habits that will help you reach your future goals. Keep going, you've got this!

FIRST SAVINGS CHALLEGE
CHALLENGE 1 : THE SMART SAVER WEEK

BEFORE YOU START

What are you giving up this week? •.......................................•

How much do you plan to save? •.......................................•

Use the table to track your cravings

S.no	Item Name	$ saved

END OF THE WEEK

# of times tempted & how did you resist?

$$ saved?

Nailed it

Challenge 2: Creative Cash-In

Now it's time to flex your creativity and find new ways to bring in some extra cash! Over the next month, think outside the box and brainstorm ways you can earn money beyond your usual income. This challenge is about showing you that there are always opportunities out there if you're willing to get a little inventive.

Whether it's selling items you no longer use, taking on extra chores around the house, or even starting a small business based on a hobby or passion, there's plenty you can do. You might have old clothes, electronics, or games you no longer need—consider selling them online or at a garage sale. If you're handy or good at something like drawing, tutoring, or even dog walking, offer your skills to neighbors, friends, or family for a little extra income. The goal here is to show you that earning money doesn't have to be boring—it can actually be fun and rewarding.

Plan It Out

Before diving in, create a simple plan. Ask yourself how much extra cash you want to earn by the end of the month and map out how you'll get there. Maybe you want to earn an extra $50 by selling items online, or maybe you've set your sights higher and want to bring in $100 by offering your skills or services. The key is to set a realistic goal, write it down, and follow through. Tracking your progress along the way will keep you motivated and give you a sense of achievement as you see your earnings grow.

Celebrate Creativity

Don't forget to share your ideas and progress with friends and family! They'll not only cheer you on but might also offer helpful suggestions or even support your efforts. Sharing your goals keeps you accountable, and having a little encouragement from people you trust can make the whole process even more enjoyable.

At the end of the month, take a moment to reflect on how your creativity paid off. You'll not only have some extra money saved up but also the satisfaction of knowing you took initiative and made it happen. This challenge is a great reminder that you have the power to create opportunities for yourself, and the skills you develop now will serve you well in the future.

FIRST SAVINGS CHALLEGE

CHALLENGE 2 : CREATIVE CASH-IN

Write down all your creative ideas..

Idea	Effort Level (Low/Medium/High)	Initial investment ($)	Potential Return ($)	Returns Type (recurring/ non-recurring)
Total :				

EXCELLENT

Challenge 3: The Entertainment Exchange

Who says having fun has to cost a fortune? In this challenge, we're swapping out pricey entertainment for budget-friendly alternatives, showing you how to enjoy life without emptying your wallet. For the next month, rethink how you spend on entertainment and challenge yourself to find cheaper, creative ways to have fun.

Instead of spending $15 on a movie ticket and another $10 on snacks, invite friends over for a movie night at home. Make popcorn, grab drinks, and create a mini-theater experience—without the steep price tag. Rather than dropping cash on amusement park tickets, explore local parks, go hiking, or visit a museum with free admission. You'd be surprised how many free or low-cost activities are out there waiting for you.

Discover Free Fun

Hunt down freebies in your area. Check out bulletin boards, websites, or apps listing local events. You might find free outdoor concerts, festivals, or art exhibits. Make a list of options and start planning your adventures. You may even discover new favorite spots.

It's not just about saving money—it's about getting creative with your free time. Try board game nights, new DIY hobbies, or cooking dinner with friends instead of eating out.

Share Experiences

Snap photos of your budget-friendly adventures and document the fun. Whether it's a nature walk or homemade pizza night, let others see that saving money doesn't mean missing out. By the end of the month, you'll have saved cash and built a list of affordable activities, realizing that budgeting doesn't equal sacrifice—it means finding new ways to enjoy life.

By the end of the month, not only will you have saved money, but you'll also have a list of go-to, affordable activities that you can enjoy anytime. You'll realize that living within a budget doesn't mean missing out—it just means finding new ways to enjoy yourself without the financial stress.

FIRST SAVINGS CHALLEGE

CHALLENGE 3 : THE ENTERTAINMENT EXCHANGE

It is possible to save & have fun!!

Here are few examples

Original Activity	Cost of Activity	Budget Friendly Alternative	Cost of Alternative	Net Gain
Going to a movie	$30	Movie night at home with friends	$5	$25
Eating out	$25	Make a new dish at home	$10	$15
Coffee Shop	$10	Iced Coffee at home	$2	$8

Original Activity	Cost of Activity	Budget Friendly Alternative	Cost of Alternative	Net Gain
	Total:		Total:	

Challenge 4: DIY Designer

Get ready to unleash your inner creative genius with the DIY Designer challenge. This is your chance to take something you've been eyeing—whether it's a new piece of clothing, room decor, or cool accessories—and make it yourself! Not only will you end up with something unique and totally customized, but you'll also save a ton of money by skipping the store. Why buy when you can DIY?

Research and Plan

Start by picking your project. Have you been wanting to upgrade your room with new decor? Or maybe you're craving a fresh wardrobe piece or a one-of-a-kind accessory? Whatever it is, your first step is research. Head online to find tutorials and inspiration. There are endless resources—YouTube, Pinterest, blogs—that can walk you through the process, no matter your skill level. Make a list of the materials you'll need, and see if you can use things you already have around the house. Gathering supplies ahead of time helps you stay organized and on budget. The goal is to get creative, not to overspend on materials!

The Fun Part: Craft Up a Storm

Once you've done your research and gathered your supplies, it's time to dive in! Put on some music, set up your workspace, and start crafting. Take your time and enjoy the process—DIY projects are all about making something that reflects your style and creativity. It might take some patience, but it'll be worth it when you see the finished product.

Showcase Your Masterpiece

Once you've completed your DIY project, don't be shy—show it off! Whether it's a custom piece of decor, a new outfit, or a funky accessory, share your creation with friends and family. Snap some pics and post them on social media, showcasing not only your creative skills but also your savvy savings. Brag a little—after all, you made something awesome and saved money in the process!

By taking on this challenge, you'll see just how much fun DIY can be, and how rewarding it feels to create something with your own hands. Plus, you'll learn valuable skills along the way that you can use for future projects. Ready to rock these challenges and level up your savings game? Let's do this!

The DIY Designer

Attach the reference picture of your project

✓ To Do

- [ ] Tutorials
- [ ] List of items required
- [ ] All items acquired

Notes

The *Future* depends on what you **Do Today**

✓ Checklist

- [ ] ....
- [ ] ....
- [ ] ....
- [ ] ....
- [ ] ....
- [ ] ....
- [ ] ....
- [ ] ....
- [ ] ....
- [ ] ....
- [ ] ....
- [ ] ....
- [ ] ....
- [ ] ....
- [ ] ....
- [ ] ....
- [ ] ....
- [ ] ....
- [ ] ....
- [ ] ....
- [ ] ....
- [ ] ....
- [ ] ....
- [ ] ....

Attach the picture of your diy project

Tips for Success

Visualize the Savings: Every time you resist an impulse buy, imagine that cash flowing into your savings account, bringing you closer to your goal. Ask your parents to help you set up a visual tracker, like a savings jar or a digital tracker, to keep you motivated and accountable.

Celebrate Small Wins: Saving money doesn't have to be all serious. For every challenge you conquer, treat yourself to a small reward, like a family movie night, extra screen time, or choosing what's for dinner. Celebrate those victories, big or small!

Group Challenges: Everything's better with friends! Invite your buddies for group savings challenges. Whether it's resisting the urge to splurge together or brainstorming creative ways to earn extra cash, making saving a social activity can boost motivation. And maybe your parents' friends can join in too!

Reflect on Values: Saving money isn't just about accumulating cash—it's about understanding what's important to you. Reflect on your values and priorities. What are your biggest goals and dreams? How does saving align with them? Having these conversations with your parents can help you stay focused on what matters most.

So, visualize those savings, celebrate your wins, rally your squad, and dive into what truly matters. With your parents by your side, there's no limit to what you can achieve!

Chapter 4:
Planning and Tracking

Welcome to a Crucial Step: Planning and Tracking Your Savings

You've set your savings goals, but how do you make sure you stay on track? Welcome to an essential part of your financial journey—planning and tracking your savings. Just like a navigator needs a map and compass to reach their destination, you need tools and methods to guide you as you save. This chapter will show you why tracking your savings is so important and introduce tools that can make the process both fun and effective.

The Importance of Tracking

Tracking your savings isn't just about keeping tabs on numbers; it's about having a clear picture of where you are on your financial journey. By tracking your progress, you can see how close you are to your goals, make adjustments when necessary, and

celebrate your achievements along the way. It's incredibly motivating to watch your savings grow over time. Every dollar saved is a step closer to reaching your goal, and tracking lets you see that progress in real time.

It also helps you stay accountable. When you know exactly how much you've saved and what's left to reach your target, it's easier to resist impulse spending or any distractions that might throw you off course. Tracking gives you control over your finances, showing you not just where you want to go but how far you've come.

Getting Started with Tracking

Ready to start? First, set some parameters for yourself. Decide what you need to track: how much you're saving, where the savings are coming from (whether it's from an allowance, gifts, or your own earnings), and any spending you need to monitor. Having a clear picture of both your income and expenses will help you stay focused.

Then, choose your tracking tools. There's no one-size-fits-all method, so find what works best for you. Some people prefer the simplicity of pen and paper, while others might like the convenience of apps that can automatically track their savings and spending. It could be as simple as writing down your progress in this book or using an app like YNAB (You Need a Budget) to give you daily updates. Whatever method you choose, make sure it's something you'll stick with.

Tools for Tracking Financial Goals

Tracking your financial goals is crucial for effective money management. In this chapter, we'll guide you on how to use this book for paper tracking and how to manage your actual savings. You'll learn the pros and cons of pulling out cash versus using a digital savings account. While some people prefer having cash on hand for a more tangible way to track their progress, others might find digital tracking easier and safer. Whichever method you choose, it's all about finding the system that makes sense for you.

Templates: Your Guide to Visual Savings Progress

This book includes templates designed to help you visually track your savings progress. These templates allow you to color in sections as you save money, giving you a clear and rewarding way to see your progress. Each template is geared toward specific savings goals, making it easy for you to get started. For example, if your goal is to save $100, the template might break it down into increments of $10 so you can see how close you're getting.

At the back of the book, you'll find more prepopulated templates tailored to common goals like saving for a vacation, buying a gadget, or building an emergency fund. These tools will help you turn saving into a visual and interactive process that keeps you motivated.

With these tools and methods in place, you're all set to start tracking your savings effectively. Not only will it help you reach your goals faster, but it will also build a foundation of financial discipline and control that will serve you throughout your life. Let's get started!

Name of the challenge

. . . .

Follow the example to keep a log of your cash savings & spendings

- When You Saved $15
- When You Saved $5
- When You Spent $10

Example

DATE	AMOUNT	TOTAL
10/10/2024	$15	$15
10/11/2024	$5	$20
10/12/2024	-$10	$10

Add

Subtract

DATE	AMOUNT	TOTAL

DATE	AMOUNT	TOTAL

Make your own Challenge!

Purpose   **Goal**

                                                   Flowers:

                                                   Leaves:

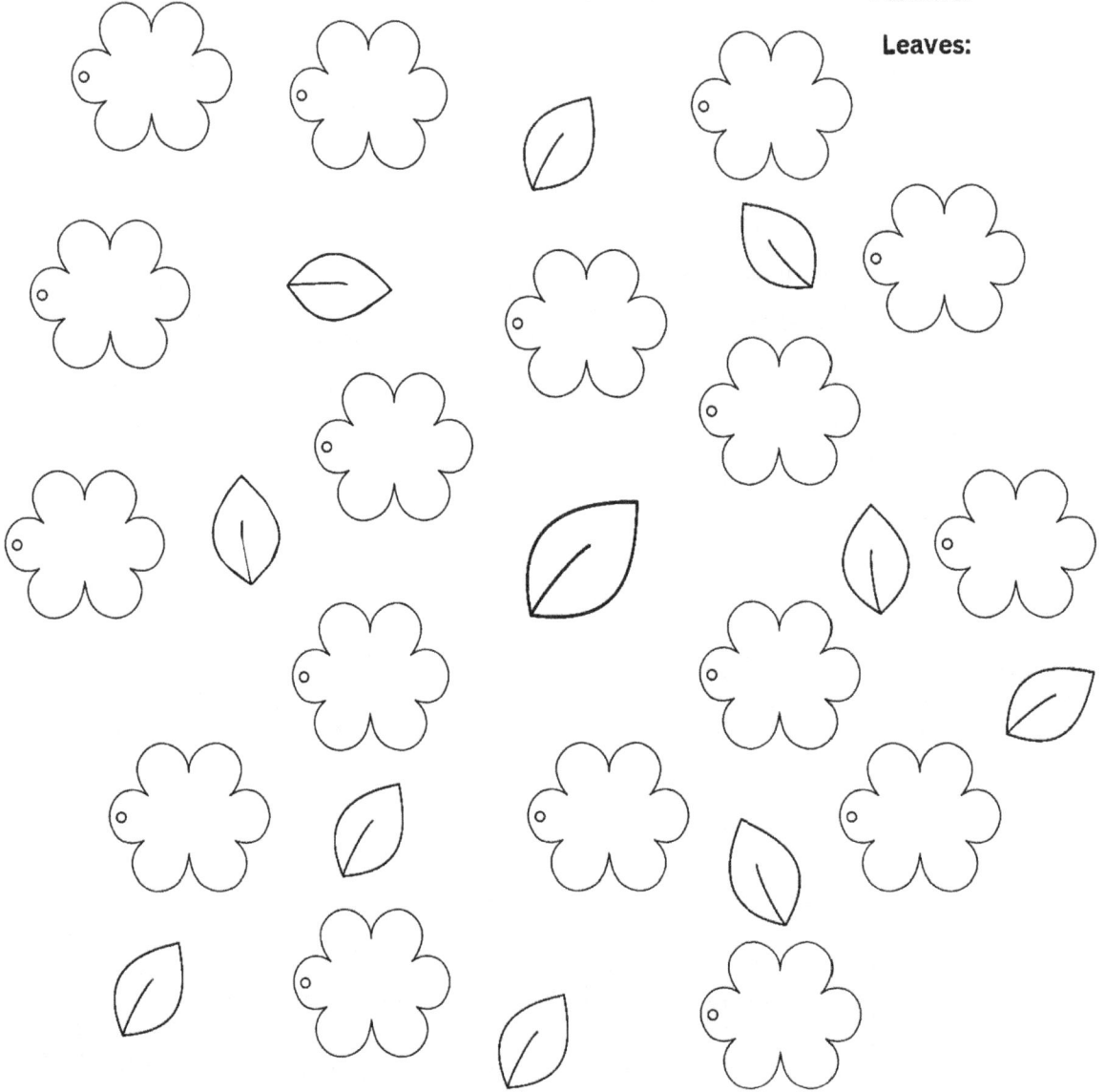

For example

If your goal is $150
Flowers (16) : each flower $5 : Total = $80
Leaves (10) : each leaf $7   : Total = $70

Digital Trackers

If you're comfortable using technology, digital tools offer a convenient and efficient way to track your savings. Here are some options you can explore:

Banking Apps: Many teen-friendly banking apps include savings trackers that automatically update your progress. They help you stay on top of your goals by sending notifications, showing your balance in real-time, and reminding you when it's time to save.

Budgeting Apps: Designed with beginners in mind, these apps allow you to set specific savings goals, track your progress, and provide reminders. Some even categorize your spending, helping you understand where your money goes and how to adjust.

Spreadsheet Templates: If you prefer more control over your tracking, spreadsheets offer a hands-on option. You can use pre-built templates or create your own to customize categories, track savings, and project your progress. This approach gives you full control over your data and allows for detailed adjustments.

Cash Tracker

For those who prefer a more tangible approach, cash tracking is a simple and visual way to manage your savings. Here's how it works:

Using Envelopes: Designate an envelope for each savings goal and store the physical cash in it. Every time you add money, record the date, amount, and new total directly on the envelope. This gives you a clear, physical representation of your savings progress.

How to Use Your Envelopes:

Label the Envelope: Clearly mark each envelope with the name of your savings goal (e.g., "Concert Tickets" or "New Laptop").

Track Deposits: Write down the date, amount, and new total every time you add to your envelope. This keeps your progress visible and organized.

Keep It Secure: Store your envelopes in a safe place, such as a locked drawer or a fireproof bag with a lock combination, to protect your cash from loss or theft.

Comparing Digital Trackers and Cash Trackers

Digital Trackers:

Pros:

Convenience: Digital tools automatically track your savings and progress. You don't have to worry about updating totals manually.

Security: Money stored in a bank or app is safe from loss, theft, or damage.

Interest Earned: Savings in a bank account can earn interest, helping your money grow over time without additional effort.

Cons:

Less Tangible: You won't physically see your money grow, which might be less motivating for visual learners.

Potential Fees: Some digital accounts or apps may charge fees or require minimum balances, so you need to stay aware of any costs.

Cash Trackers:

Pros:

Tangible Progress: You can physically see and touch your savings, which can be highly motivating, especially if you're a visual learner.

Simple to Use: There's no need for apps, bank accounts, or technology—just you, an envelope, and your savings.

Cons:

Risk of Loss or Theft: Physical cash can be lost, stolen, or damaged, so it's important to store it securely.

No Interest Earned: Unlike digital savings accounts, cash in an envelope doesn't earn interest, so your money doesn't grow passively.

Less Practical for Large Amounts: Storing large sums of cash can be cumbersome and potentially unsafe.

Which Method is Right for You?

Both digital and cash tracking have their benefits and challenges, so it comes down to personal preference and what works best for your lifestyle. Digital trackers provide convenience, security, and the potential for earning interest, while cash tracking offers a tangible, hands-on way to watch your savings grow. If you enjoy physically seeing your progress, the cash method might be more motivating. If you prefer simplicity and security, a digital tracker could be the better option. The important thing is to pick a method that helps you stay committed to your goals and keeps you motivated on your savings journey!

Name of the challenge

....

Follow the example to keep a log of your cash savings & spendings

Example

- When You Saved $15
- When You Saved $5
- When You Spent $10

DATE	AMOUNT	TOTAL
10/10/2024	$15	$15
10/11/2024	$5	$20
10/12/2024	-$10	$10

Add / Subtract

DATE	AMOUNT	TOTAL

DATE	AMOUNT	TOTAL

Money Skills for Teens and Young Adults

DIGITAL SAVINGS TRACKER

CHECK BOOK

NAME OF THE
DEPOSITOR: ....

SAVING FOR: ....

Keep a track of all your Digital Savings

DEPOSIT DATE	DIGITAL SOURCE	AMOUNT DEPOSITED (+)	AMOUNT SPENT (-)	NET SAVINGS

Journaling Your Progress

Beyond tracking numbers, keeping a savings journal can be a powerful tool to reflect on your financial journey. Writing about your experiences with spending and saving can give you insight into your habits and help you identify areas for improvement. Start with daily reflections where you note any challenges, victories, or new strategies you discover along the way. This kind of self-awareness can help you adjust your approach and stay focused.

As you reach milestones in your savings goals, use your journal to celebrate those achievements. Reflect on what hitting these goals means to you and how it's bringing you closer to your bigger financial aspirations. Journaling isn't just about writing down numbers—it's about acknowledging the effort you're putting in and reinforcing your commitment.

Creating a Habit

Consistency is key when it comes to tracking your savings. To build a solid habit, set aside a regular time each week to update your tracker. This could be a quiet moment alone to reflect on your progress or a shared activity with a friend or family member who's also working on their savings goals. Regularly updating your tracker not only keeps you organized but also helps you stay motivated by reminding you of the progress you're making.

Tips for Effective Tracking

Start with a simple tracking method that feels manageable. Whether you're using pen and paper or a digital tool, keeping it straightforward will make it easier to stay consistent. As you become more comfortable with the process, you can always add more detail or complexity to your tracking system.

Be honest with yourself during the process. It's normal to have setbacks, but the key is learning from them and adjusting your approach. Tracking isn't about perfection; it's about progress.

Regular reviews are also important. Set aside time to review your tracker, make adjustments to your goals if needed, and plan for the future. Celebrating your progress along the way—whether it's reaching a milestone or simply sticking to your plan—can be a powerful motivator to keep going. Acknowledging how far you've come reinforces your commitment and builds confidence for the journey ahead.

By using this book to both track your savings on paper and manage your money, whether in cash or digitally, you'll stay organized, motivated, and well on your way to financial success.

Chapter 5:
Medium-Term Savings Challenges

Mastering Medium-Term Savings Challenges

After mastering short-term savings, it's time to tackle medium-term challenges. These challenges will push you to save over a longer period—weeks or even months—helping you develop persistence and adaptability. As you work through these challenges, you'll strengthen your savings habits and grow more confident in managing your money. Here's how you can level up your savings game with a series of incremental challenges:

Challenge 1: The 30-Day Savings Sprint

For the next 30 days, commit to saving a fixed percentage of any money you receive, such as allowance, gift money, or income from odd jobs. Start with a manageable percentage, like 30%.

Plan: Decide how you'll track the money you receive and set aside for savings.

Execute: Transfer your savings to a separate account or savings jar immediately upon receiving money. Stay diligent throughout the month.

Reward: At the end of the month, review your progress. Treat yourself to something small, but keep the majority in savings to stay on track.

Challenge 2: The No-Spend Challenge (Weekend Edition)

Pick one weekend each month where you don't spend any money. This means planning ahead for meals, entertainment, and other needs.

Prepare: Plan your meals, gather supplies, and prepare for activities that cost nothing.

Engage: Enjoy cost-free activities, like nature walks, game nights, or DIY projects.

Reflect: Write about the experience in your journal. Was it difficult? What did you learn about your spending habits?

Challenge 3: The Big Save

Choose one monthly or bimonthly expense (like a subscription service or dining out) and cut it out for two months. Redirect that money into your savings.

Identify: Choose a non-essential expense that's challenging but not necessary.

Strategy: Plan how you'll replace this item or activity with a free or low-cost alternative.

Celebrate: At the end of the challenge, reward yourself with a small treat from the savings but keep the rest saved.

Challenge 4: Match It

Every time you spend money on non-essential items, match the amount by putting the same amount into savings. This helps you think critically about every purchase.

Track: Keep a detailed log of your non-essential spending and the matching savings.

Balance: Review the log each week. How does your spending compare to your savings?

Reward: If you successfully match or exceed your spending with savings, treat yourself to a small reward.

Building Recognition and Rewards

Staying motivated is key, and rewards play a big part in keeping you on track. For every challenge you complete, give yourself points and unlock rewards based on how many you've earned. These rewards should be fun but still in line with your savings goals.

Ideas for rewards include:

10 Points: A low-cost activity like a movie night at home or a favorite treat.

20 Points: A small purchase, like a new book or game.

30 Points: A shopping trip with friends, using a predetermined budget.

Sharing Your Success

Don't keep your progress to yourself! Share your achievements with supportive friends or family members, or post your progress on social media. Sharing your journey can inspire others to start their own savings goals, and it creates a community of savers who motivate one another. Remember, these medium-term challenges are not just about the money—they're about building lifelong habits of financial responsibility and independence. Every challenge you complete brings you closer to long-term financial success.

Chapter 6:
Long-Term Savings Goals

Embarking on long-term savings goals is like setting off on an epic journey. It requires preparation, determination, and the ability to look beyond the immediate future. These goals often involve saving significant amounts of money over a longer period, such as saving for college, a car, or even a dream vacation. This chapter will guide you through the process of setting, planning for, and committing to your long-term savings goals.

Understanding Long-Term Savings Goals

Long-term savings goals typically take years to achieve and can have a significant impact on your life. These goals provide opportunities, security, and the chance to fulfill dreams. Because of their scope, it's important to take a strategic approach to ensure you stay on track over time.

Setting Your Goal

Define Clearly: Be specific about what you're saving for. Instead of a vague goal like "save for college," aim for something more detailed like "save $10,000 for college expenses before high school graduation."

Research Costs: Understand how much your goal will realistically cost, factoring in inflation or potential cost increases, especially for goals several years down the road.

Establish a Time Frame: Set a deadline for when you'd like to achieve your goal. This helps you determine how much you need to save each month or year to stay on track.

Planning for Your Goal

Break It Down: Large savings goals can feel overwhelming. Break them into smaller, manageable targets—yearly, monthly, or even weekly. This makes the process more digestible and less daunting.

Choose the Right Tools: For long-term goals, consider using savings accounts with higher interest rates, certificates of deposit (CDs), or even investment accounts. The longer your time frame, the more you can benefit from compound interest.

Automate Your Savings: Set up automatic transfers to your savings account. This "set it and forget it" approach ensures you consistently save without having to think about it every time. Automation makes saving easier and more reliable.

Challenges Tailored to Long-Term Commitments

Incorporate challenges to keep yourself motivated during the long-term savings process. Here are a few ideas to help you stay focused and disciplined:

The Incremental Increase Challenge: Start by saving a small amount and gradually increase it each month. For example, save $50 in the first month and increase it to $55 the next month. These small increments will add up over time without feeling overwhelming.

The Extra Income Challenge: Find ways to earn extra money and dedicate those earnings directly to your savings. This could come from side jobs, selling unused items, or offering services like tutoring or design work.

The Substitute Spending Challenge: Identify one non-essential spending habit, such as dining out or a subscription service, and cut it out for a set period. Redirect the money you save into your long-term savings goal.

Staying Motivated

Long-term goals require perseverance, but staying motivated is key to success. Here are some strategies to help you stay on track:

Visualize Your Goal: Create a visual representation of your goal, like a poster or vision board, that you see everyday. This will serve as a constant reminder of what you're working toward.

Celebrate Milestones: Break your larger goal into smaller milestones, such as saving your first $1,000 or reaching the halfway point. Celebrate each milestone as you achieve it to maintain motivation.

Adjust as Needed: Life can change, and so can your goals. Regularly review your progress and adjust your plan if needed to ensure it still aligns with your priorities and time frame.

Adding the Family Match Challenge

A great way to accelerate your savings and involve your family in your financial journey is through the **Family Match Challenge**. This challenge not only helps grow your savings but also encourages your family to support your financial goals.

Step 1: Present Your Goal

Share your savings goal with your family. Explain what you're saving for, why it's important to you, and how you plan to achieve it. This helps your family understand the value of supporting your journey.

Step 2: Propose the Challenge

Ask a family member to match a portion of your savings. It doesn't have to be dollar-for-dollar—even a small match, like 25 cents for every dollar you save, can make a significant difference.

Step 3: Set the Terms

Agree on the specifics of the challenge:

> **Matching Rate:** Decide how much your family will contribute for each dollar you save.
>
> **Duration:** Determine how long the challenge will last or until you reach a specific milestone.
>
> **Maximum Contribution:** Set a cap on the total amount your family will match.

Step 4: Track Your Progress

Keep a record of your savings and your family's contributions. You can use a shared spreadsheet, a savings app, or a physical chart at home. Regular updates keep everyone informed and excited about reaching your goal.

Step 5: Celebrate Milestones Together

When you reach significant milestones, celebrate with your family. These celebrations reinforce the value of discipline, effort, and shared achievement.

Benefits of the Family Match Challenge

Accelerates Savings: Matching contributions can speed up how quickly you reach your goal.

Fosters Team Spirit: Working together strengthens family bonds and creates a sense of shared accomplishment.

Educates: This challenge provides a hands-on lesson in the power of saving and collective effort.

Motivates: Knowing that your family is invested in your success can be a powerful incentive to keep saving.

Involving Your Family in Your Financial Goals

Involving your family in your financial goals is a great way to strengthen support and create shared accountability. When you bring them into your savings journey, you open up conversations about money, helping everyone learn and grow together. It's not just about accelerating your savings; it's about building trust and creating a sense of teamwork. Your family can offer advice, encouragement, and even help celebrate your milestones along the way. By making them part of your financial journey, you're fostering a supportive environment that benefits everyone, while reinforcing the importance of financial responsibility. This collaborative effort helps create lasting habits that not only help you reach your goals but also instill a culture of smart saving and planning within your family.

Chapter 7:
Creative Saving Tips

Finding ways to save money can be a bit different for teens and tweens, especially if you don't have a steady income yet. But don't worry—there are plenty of creative strategies to boost your savings without needing a big paycheck. This chapter is all about fun, clever ways to save, helping you make the most of the money you get from allowances, gifts, or occasional jobs.

The Change Jar Adventure

Start a change jar for any cash you receive. Whenever you get money from chores or gifts, drop some coins or $1 bills into the jar. You'll be surprised how quickly small amounts add up over time.

The 48-Hour Wishlist Rule

When you see something you want, add it to a wishlist and wait 48 hours before deciding. If you still want it after two days and it fits within your savings goals, consider saving up for it specifically.

DIY Crafts and Gifts

Instead of buying gifts or room decor, try making them. There are tons of online tutorials for DIY crafts, decorations, and thoughtful homemade gifts that save money and add a personal touch.

Entertainment on a Budget

Find free or low-cost entertainment options. Organize game nights, have movie marathons at home, or explore free community events. Many museums and zoos also offer free admission days.

Savvy Shopping for Games and Apps

Wait for sales before buying new games or look for second-hand games in good condition. Use free versions of apps when possible, and think twice before making in-app purchases.

Utilize Student Discounts

Take advantage of student discounts on activities, software, and clothing. Always ask about available discounts before making a purchase.

Challenge Your Friends

Make saving a game by challenging your friends to save money too. See who can save the most over a month or who can come up with the most creative saving idea. Saving with friends makes it more fun and competitive.

Learn to Cook Simple Meals

Eating out or ordering in can quickly drain your savings. Learning to cook simple, tasty meals at home can save you money and serve you well beyond your teen years.

Repair and Upcycle

Before throwing something out or buying a new item, see if it can be repaired or upcycled. There are plenty of ideas online for turning old t-shirts into bags, jeans into shorts, or even revamping furniture.

Save Smart on School Supplies

School supplies can be a big expense each year. Save by buying in bulk, reusing items from the previous year, or swapping supplies with friends. Be on the lookout for back-to-school sales too.

The best saving strategies are the ones you enjoy and can stick to—when saving feels like a fun challenge rather than a chore. Personalize your approach based on what excites you and aligns with your goals. Whether you're saving for a new video game, concert tickets, or something bigger in the future, every little bit adds up and brings you closer to where you want to be. Remember, saving and managing your money is a marathon, not a sprint. Build smart money habits now, and your future self will thank you.

Monthly Savings Challenge for Food and Drinks

Week 1: Awareness

Objective: Track every cent spent on food and drinks.
Action: Keep a detailed diary or use a budget tracking app to record your expenses.
Goal: Gain a clear understanding of your current spending patterns.

Week 2: Set a Budget

Objective: Reduce spending by 10% compared to last week.
Action: For example, if you spend $5 daily on snacks or drinks, aim to limit it to $4.50.
Goal: Start small to ease into the changes without feeling deprived.

Week 3: Alternative Choices

Objective: Explore lower-cost alternatives for food and drinks.
Action: Try cheaper places, look for promotions, or prepare homemade meals or drinks twice this week.
Goal: Compare satisfaction and savings from these budget-friendly alternatives.

Week 4: Increase Homemade Intake

Objective: Prepare more homemade food and drinks.
Action: Increase the number of homemade meals to four times this week.
Goal: Notice the difference in spending and discover new favorite recipes.

Month-End Review

Objective: Analyze your savings and adjust your habits accordingly.
Action: Review the month's spending on food and drinks and assess the impact of your efforts.
Goal: Decide if the new spending level is sustainable and enjoyable, then set a savings target for the next month.

Savings Milestones

$25 Saved: Reward yourself with a small treat (like a fancy coffee or dessert).
$50 Saved: Use it for a personal expense or keep it for future needs.
$100 Saved: Celebrate this major milestone—consider investing in quality meal prep tools or equipment to help you save even more.

Ongoing Tips

Bulk Buying: Purchase drinks and snacks in bulk from a grocery store rather than a gas station or vending machine.
Loyalty Programs: Join loyalty programs at your favorite coffee shops to earn rewards or discounts.

Weekly Prep: Set aside time each week to meal prep, reducing the temptation to buy lunch or snacks on busy days.

Saving on Clothing and Fashion Challenge

Week 1: Closet Inventory

Objective: Take stock of what you already own.
Action: Organize your closet and identify items you truly need.
Goal: Avoid duplicate purchases and pinpoint items to sell or donate.

Week 2: Smart Shopping Strategies

Objective: Make smart purchases and find great deals.
Action: Use coupons, shop out of season, and visit thrift stores.
Goal: Focus on thoughtful purchases that offer real value for your money.

Week 3: DIY Fashion

Objective: Customize or repair your existing clothes.
Action: Learn basic sewing or customization techniques to refresh your wardrobe.
Goal: Extend the life of your clothes and reduce the need to buy new ones.

Week 4: Fashion Budget Review

Objective: Evaluate your new clothing spending habits.
Action: Compare this month's spending to previous months.
Goal: Determine if your new shopping habits are sustainable and fulfilling.

Entertainment & Subscriptions Management

Week 1: Audit Your Subscriptions

Objective: Identify all subscriptions you're paying for.
Action: List every subscription service (streaming, apps, magazines) and their costs.
Goal: Understand your total monthly spending on these services.

Week 2: Cut Unnecessary Subscriptions

Objective: Reduce unnecessary subscription expenses.
Action: Cancel any subscription you haven't used in the past month.
Goal: Simplify and keep only what you use regularly.

Week 3: Share Costs

Objective: Share subscription benefits and costs with others.
Action: Share streaming services with friends or family where possible, following legal guidelines.
Goal: Reduce individual costs by sharing accounts.

Week 4: Subscription Savings Analysis

Objective: Review the financial impact of cutting and sharing subscriptions.
Action: Calculate your total savings from reducing or sharing subscriptions.
Goal: Commit to keeping only the most valuable services.

Optimizing Holiday and Gift Expenses

Week 1: Budgeting for Gifts

Objective: Set a realistic budget for holiday spending.
Action: List everyone you plan to buy gifts for and allocate a specific amount to each person.
Goal: Prepare for holiday expenses without overspending.

Week 2: Creative Gift Solutions

Objective: Reduce gift expenses with personalized gifts.
Action: Use your skills to craft gifts, bake treats, or create art.
Goal: Deliver thoughtful gifts that cost less and have more meaning.

Week 3: Group Gifts and Shared Costs

Objective: Collaborate on gift-giving.
Action: Organize group gifts for common friends or family members to share costs.
Goal: Maximize the impact of your gifts while minimizing individual expenses.

Week 4: Post-Holiday Expense Review

Objective: Reflect on your holiday spending.
Action: Review how much you spent versus what you budgeted.
Goal: Learn from this year's experience to plan better for next year.

Encouragement for Setbacks

"Every setback is a setup for a comeback. Keep saving!": Setbacks are normal and part of the process—what matters is continuing the journey.

"Adjust your strategies, not your goal.": If a challenge is tough, tweak your approach rather than abandoning your goal.

"Progress over perfection.": Focus on steady progress rather than striving for perfection.

"Small steps lead to big results.": Celebrate each small win, knowing it all adds up.

"Learn from every mistake.": View mistakes as learning opportunities, not failures.

"Consistency is key.": Regular saving, even in small amounts, builds long-term success.

"Believe in your journey.": Stay committed and trust the process, even when it feels slow.

"Every dollar saved is a step closer to your dream.": Keep your eyes on the end goal, knowing each bit of savings brings you closer.

Conclusion:
Your Financial Journey Begins

Congratulations on completing the Teen Money Skills Challenge! You've taken the first important steps toward mastering your finances. By learning how to manage money, differentiate between wants and needs, and plan for real-world expenses, you're setting yourself up for a future of financial freedom.

Remember, financial literacy is a lifelong journey. The skills and habits you've developed through interactive challenges in this book will continue to benefit you as you grow. Keep practicing what you've learned, and don't be afraid to revisit the exercises to sharpen your skills.

As you move forward, remember these key points:

Set Clear Goals: Always have a financial target in mind, whether it's saving for a big purchase or building an emergency fund.

Stay Disciplined: Stick to your budgets and savings plans. It's okay to treat yourself occasionally, but keep your long-term goals in focus.

Learn and Adapt: The financial world is always changing. Stay curious, keep learning, and adapt your strategies as needed.

You now have the tools to make smart financial decisions and avoid the debt and financial struggles that many adults face. Share your knowledge with friends and family, and continue to build on what you've learned.

Your journey to financial independence has just begun. Embrace it with confidence, and remember—you have the power to shape your financial future.

Savings Challenge Templates

One of the best ways to take control of your money is to have a plan for it. It's not just about saving randomly, but about deciding where every dollar goes so you can enjoy the things you want, without stress. Learning how to set savings goals and stick to them helps you ensure that your money works for you, not vice versa.

When you set a goal-saving for something fun or just building up your savings—breaking it down into smaller, manageable steps makes the process a lot easier. Instead of thinking, "I need to save $500," you can focus on saving $20 or $50 at a time. Each small step you take gets you closer to your goal, and before you know it, you'll have what you need without feeling overwhelmed.

The important thing is to always be prepared. Having a savings plan in place means you're ready for whatever comes up, whether it's an unexpected opportunity or a surprise expense. You won't have to scramble to find money at the last minute or miss out on something because you weren't ready. By learning to plan and save now,

you're setting yourself up to handle bigger financial goals in the future—like travel, emergencies, or major life events—without the stress of not being prepared.

The great thing about these savings challenges is that they teach you discipline and give you the freedom to enjoy yourself without the guilt of overspending. It's all about balance: making sure you're smart with your money while still having fun. And the best part is, this is a skill you'll take with you throughout your life. Learning how to tell your money where to go instead of wondering where it went will help you in every stage of life, from school to your first job, and beyond.

Going Out Fund (Movies, Dining, Events, Dating)

$20-$25: Movie Ticket with Popcorn and a Drink

Movies and Snacks: A movie t`icket combined with popcorn and a drink usually costs $20-$25. This is perfect for teens wanting to catch a blockbuster with friends. Matinee showings often offer cheaper tickets, allowing for more snack money.

$40-$50: Dinner at a Mid-Range or Trendy Restaurant

Dining Experience: A night out at a popular mid-range or trendy restaurant can range from $40 to $50. Splitting the bill with friends makes it more affordable while still enjoying a quality meal.

$60: Entry Fees for Activities Like an Escape Room or Amusement Park

Escape Rooms: Interactive experiences like escape rooms charge $30-$60 per person, great for group adventures.

Amusement Parks: Entry to local amusement parks usually falls around $60 for a day pass, offering hours of rides and fun.

$100: Tickets to a Concert or Special Event

Concerts: General admission tickets to concerts or events like sports games can cost around $100. Extra expenses like transportation and snacks should be considered.

$100: Day Trip with Friends to a Nearby Attraction

Nearby Getaways: A fun day trip to local attractions with meals and transportation included can fit within a $100 budget. Carpooling helps reduce transportation costs.

$150: More Extensive Day Trip with Friends

Adventure Day: A $150 budget allows for a more adventurous day trip, including transportation, meals, and activities like mini-golf or a larger theme park.

$200: Mini-Festival Experience with Friends

Music or Food Festivals: Attending a small music or food festival can range from $150 to $200, including tickets, snacks, and transportation. Group discounts can make it more affordable.

Dont let the money hold you back this time while going out

Going Out Fund

HAVE FUN

$5

$7

$15

Movie Theatre ($25)

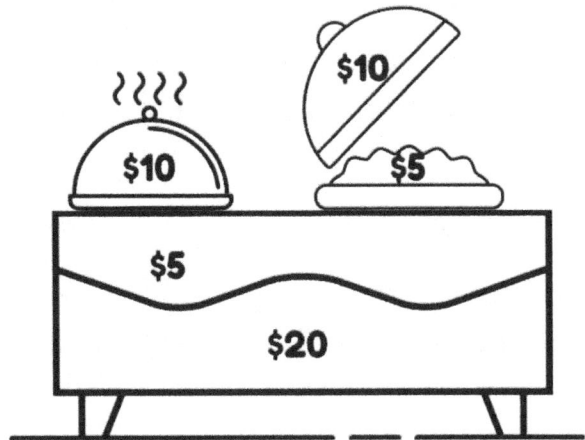

$10

$10

$5

$5

$20

Trendy Restaurant ($50)

$20

EXIT

$5

$5

$10

$10 $10

Escape Room ($60)

$25 CONCERT

$10

$15

$30

$20 LIVE

Music Concert ($100)

Money Skills for Teens and Young Adults

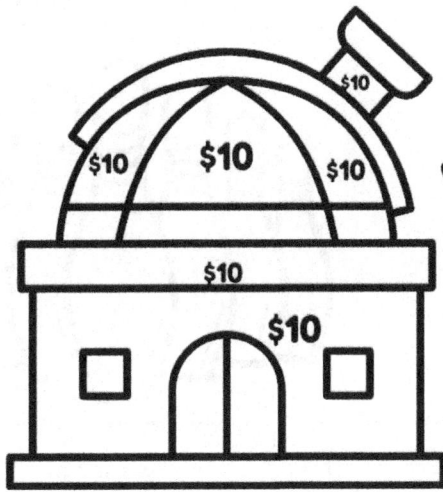

$10
$10
$10
$10
$10
$10

ZOO $10
$10
$10
$10

Extensive Day Trip

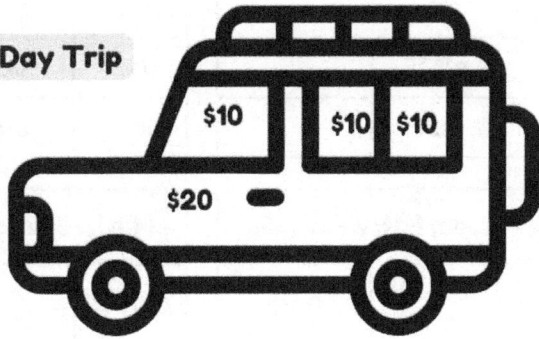

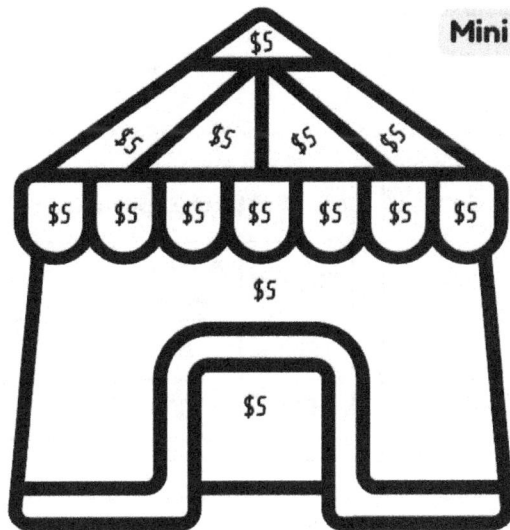

$5
$10
$10
$5
$5
$10

$10
$10
$10

$20

$10
$10

Mini Festival Experiance

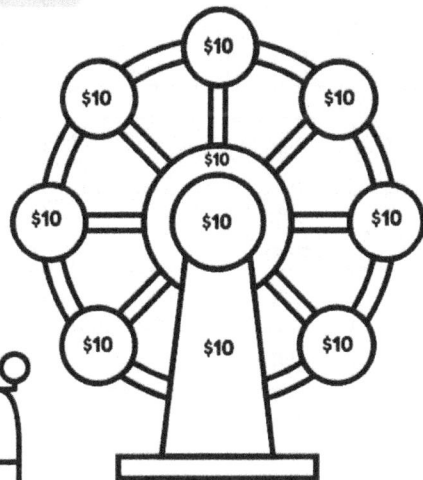

$5
$5
$5
$5
$5
$5
$5
$5
$5
$5
$5
$5
$5
$5

$5

$10
$10
$10
$10
$10
$10
$10
$10
$10
$10

$5

$5
$10

Going Out Fund Log

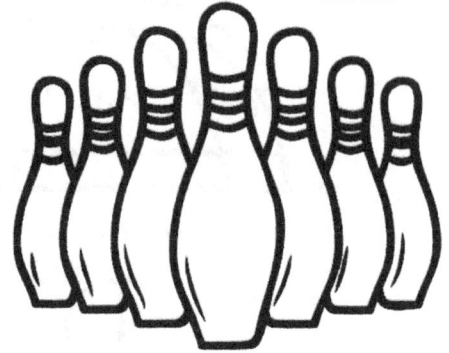

Movie ($20-$25)

%Saved	Amount Saved	Date
25%	$6.25	
50%	$12.5	
75%	$18.75	
100%	$25	

Trendy Restaurant ($40-$50)

%Saved	Amount Saved	Date
25%	$12.5	
50%	$25	
75%	$18.75	
100%	$50	

List of Favorites

Movie : ....

Restaurant : ....

Sports / Game : ....

Music Album : ....

Tourist place : ....
(local)

Tourist place : ....
(non-local)

Coffee Shop: ....

Escape Room Entry Fee ($60)

%Saved	Amount Saved	Date
25%	$15	
50%	$30	
75%	$45	
100%	$60	

Music/Special Event ($100)

%Saved	Amount Saved	Date
25%	$25	
50%	$50	
75%	$75	
100%	$100	

Day Trip ($100)

%Saved	Amount Saved	Date
25%	$25	
50%	$50	
75%	$75	
100%	$100	

Extensive Trip ($150)

%Saved	Amount Saved	Date
25%	$37.5	
50%	$75	
75%	$112.5	
100%	$150	

Mini Festival Experience ($200)

%Saved	Amount Saved	Date
25%	$50	
50%	$100	
75%	$150	
100%	$200	

Car Savings Fund

Get Excited About Your Car Savings Journey!

Embarking on the journey to save for a car isn't just about reaching a financial goal; it's about unlocking the freedom and independence that come with car ownership. By setting clear milestones, you'll stay motivated and gain valuable insights into the true costs of owning and maintaining a vehicle. Each milestone represents a crucial aspect of car ownership, helping you prepare for the exciting road ahead.

$50: Gas Refill

Fueling Up: This initial milestone helps cover the cost of a full gas tank, essential for keeping the car running and ensuring you're always ready to hit the road.

$100: Cleaning Services

Professional Cleaning: Save $100 for a professional car wash and detailing to maintain both the aesthetic and hygiene of your vehicle, ensuring it always looks and feels fresh.

$200: Standard Maintenance

Regular Upkeep: Allocate $200 for regular maintenance such as oil changes, fluid checks, or minor repairs to keep your car running smoothly and efficiently.

$350: Monthly Insurance

Insurance Coverage: Set aside $350 to cover one month's insurance premium, an essential cost to protect your vehicle from damages, accidents, and theft.

$500: Tire Replacement

New Tires: Save $500 for a full set of tires, ensuring your vehicle has the traction and safety needed to navigate various road conditions and maintain optimal performance.

$750: Emergency Reserve

Unexpected Repairs: Establish an emergency fund with $750 to cover unexpected major repairs, such as brake or suspension work, so you're financially prepared for surprises.

$1,000: Annual Gas Budget

Fuel Costs: Save $1,000 to manage a year's worth of gasoline, ensuring you have an ongoing budget to handle one of the largest regular expenses for vehicle operation.

$1,500: Audio System Upgrade

Entertainment Enhancement: Consider investing $1,500 into a high-quality audio system, providing a more enjoyable driving experience with upgraded sound for music and entertainment.

$2,500: Initial Ownership Costs

Insurance and Registration: Set aside $2,500 to cover the initial costs of insurance, registration, and taxes when purchasing a new or used vehicle.

$3,500: Comprehensive Repair Fund

Major Repairs: Prepare $3,500 for more significant repairs such as engine or gearbox issues. This fund ensures that unexpected breakdowns don't derail your budget.

$4,500: Vehicle Technology Enhancements

Tech Upgrades: Allocate $4,500 for advanced vehicle technology upgrades such as a navigation system, rear-view cameras, or automated safety features to enhance both safety and convenience.

$5,000: Purchase Down Payment

Vehicle Purchase: The ultimate savings goal of $5,000 can be used as a down payment, significantly lowering your monthly payments or helping you purchase a car outright, making it a key milestone for ownership.

Save for your Car

Your dream car is just few miles away

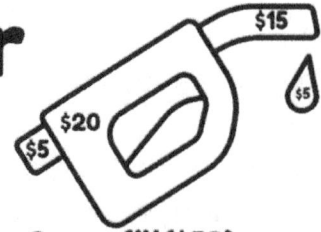
Gas refill ($50)

$15
$5
$20
$5

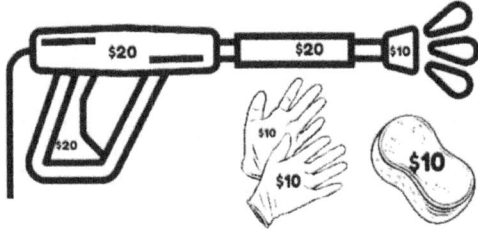
$20 $20 $10
$20
$10
$10
$10
Cleaning services ($100)

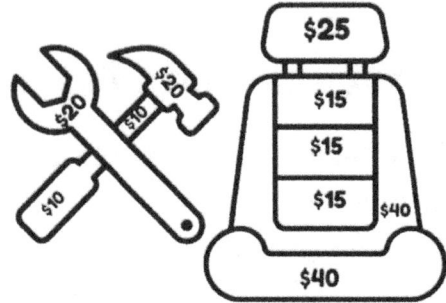
$25
$20
$10
$20
$15
$15
$15
$10
$40
$40
Standard Maintenance ($200)

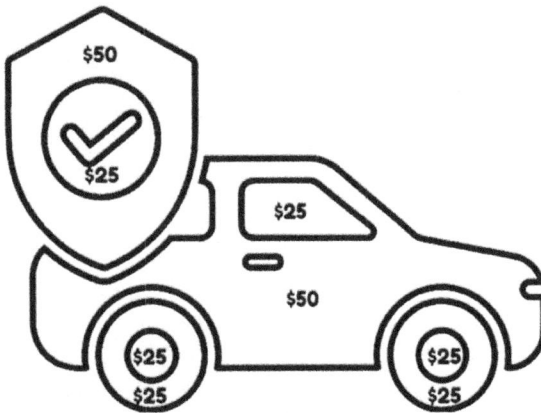
$50
$25
$25
$25
$25
$25
$25
Monthly insurance ($250)

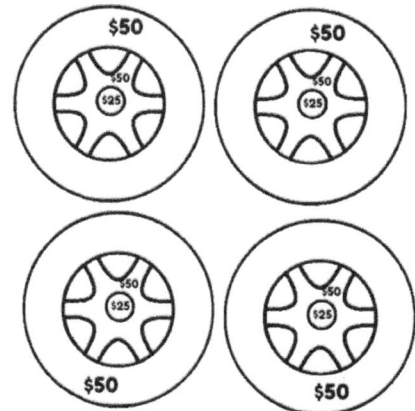
$50 $50
$50 $50
$25 $25
$50 $50
$50 $50
$25 $25
$50 $50
Tire Replacement ($500)

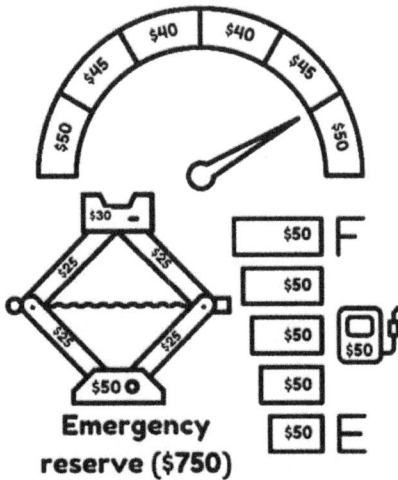
$40 $40
$45 $45
$50 $50
$30
$25 $25
$25 $25
$50
$50 F
$50
$50
$50
$50 E
Emergency reserve ($750)

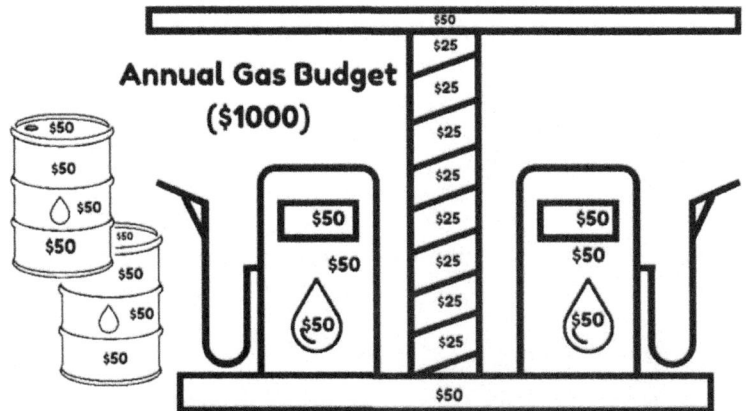
$50
$50
$50
$50
$50
$50
Annual Gas Budget ($1000)
$50
$25
$25
$25
$25
$25
$50
$50
$25
$25
$50
$50
$50

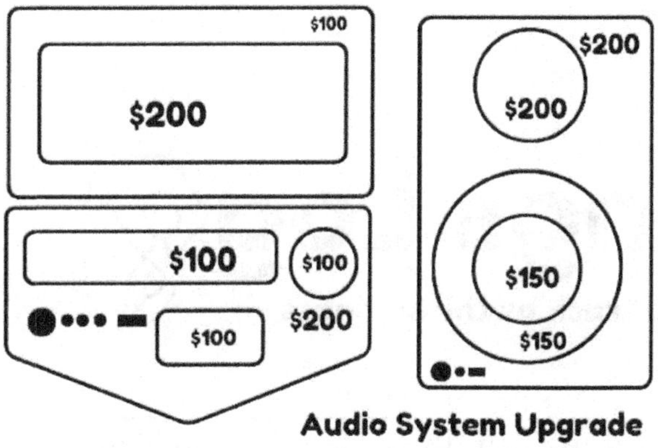

Audio System Upgrade
($1500)

Initial ownership costs ($2500)

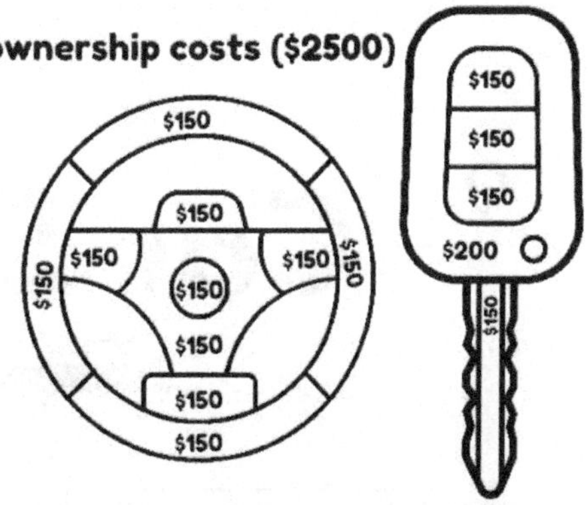

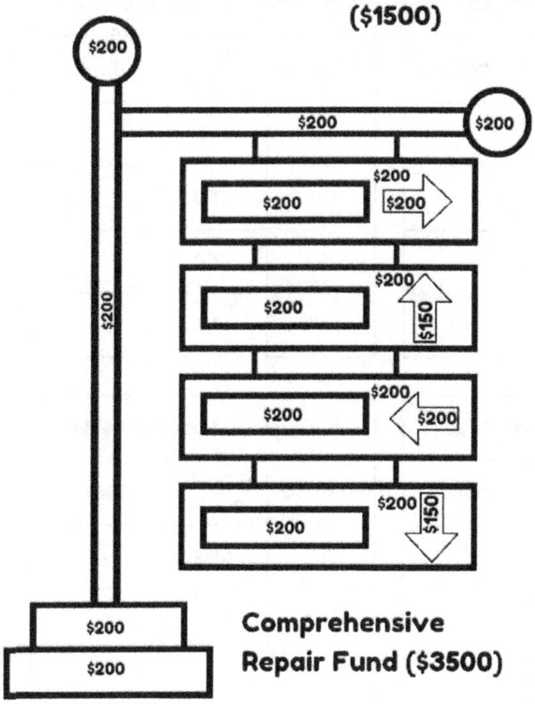

Comprehensive
Repair Fund ($3500)

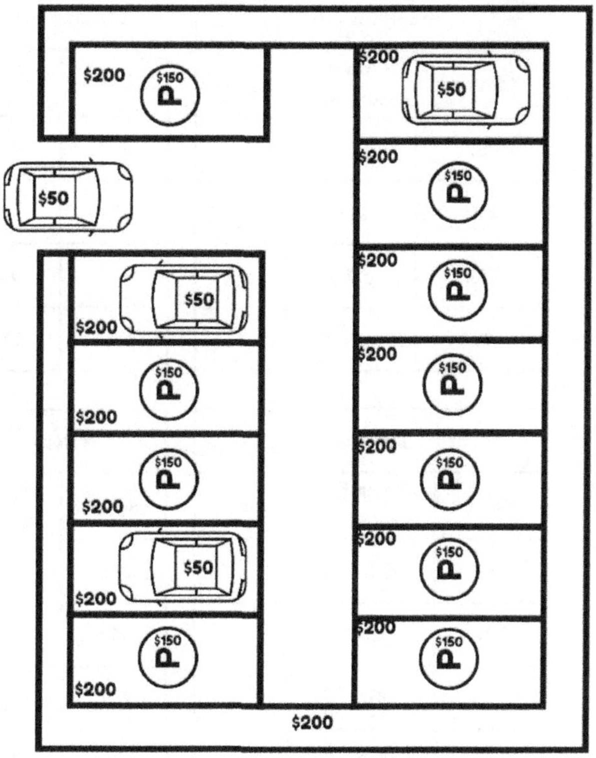

Vehicle Technology
Enhancements ($4500)

Purchase Down Payment
($5000)

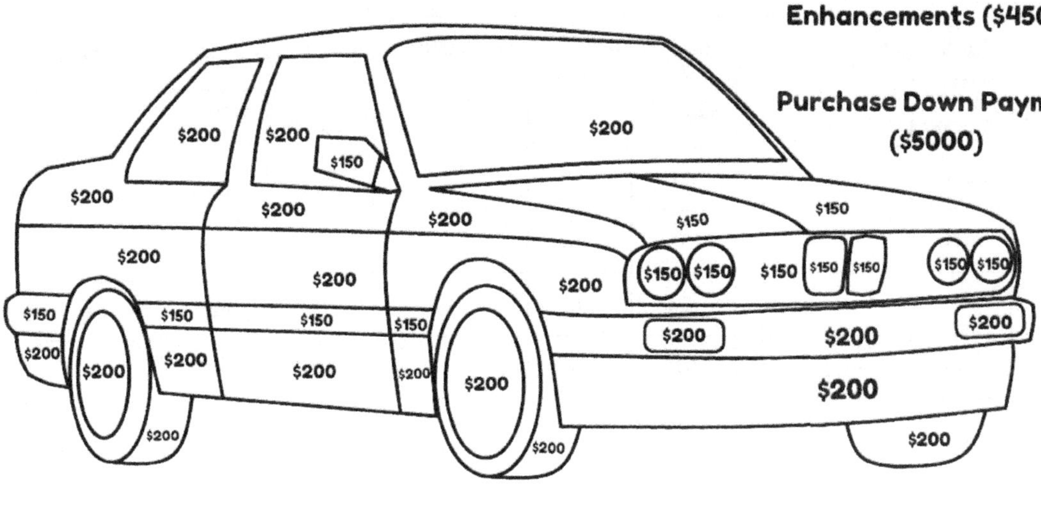

Car Savings Log

Keep a track of the savingss

Gas Refill - $50		
% Saved	Amount Saved	Date
25%	$12.5	
50%	$25	
75%	$37.5	
100%	$50	

Cleaning Services - $100		
% Saved	Amount Saved	Date
25%	25	
50%	50	
75%	75	
100%	100	

Standard Maintenance - $200		
%Saved	Amount Saved	Date
25%	$50	
50%	$100	
75%	$150	
100%	$200	

Monthly Insurance - $250		
%Saved	Amount Saved	Date
25%	$63~	
50%	$125	
75%	$187.5	
100%	$250	

Tire Replacement - $500		
%Saved	Amount Saved	Date
25%	$125	
50%	$250	
75%	$375	
100%	$500	

Emergency Reserve - $750		
%Saved	Amount Saved	Date
25%	$188	
50%	$375	
75%	$563~	
100%	$750	

Annual Gas Budget - $1000		
%Saved	Amount Saved	Date
25%	$250	
50%	$500	
75%	$750	
100%	$1000	

Audio System Upgrage - $1500		
%Saved	Amount Saved	Date
25%	$375	
50%	$750	
75%	$1125	
100%	$1500	

Initial Ownership Costs - $2500		
%Saved	Amount Saved	Date
25%	$625	
50%	$1250	
75%	$1875	
100%	$2500	

Money Skills for Teens and Young Adults

Comprehensive Repair Fund – $3500		
% saved	Amount Saved	Date
25%	$875	
50%	$1750	
75%	$2625	
100%	$3500	

Vehicle Technology Enhancements – $4500		
%Saved	Amount Saved	Date
	$1125	
	$2250	
	$3375	
	$4500	

Purchase Down-payment – $5000		
%Saved	Amount Saved	Date
	$1250	
	$2500	
	$3750	
	$5000	

Color the fuel indicator level as you complete sub challenges in this journey..

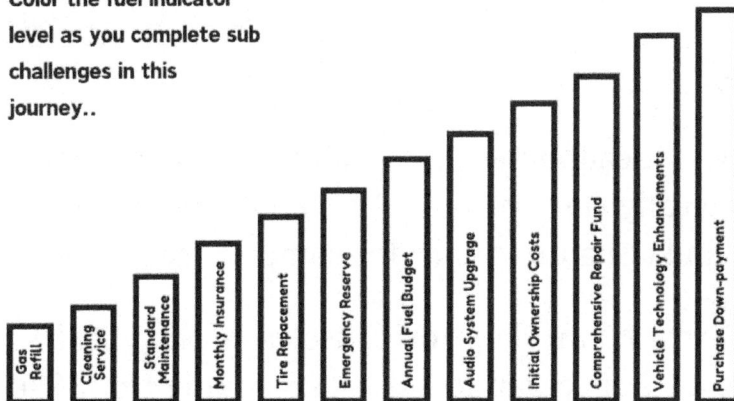

The car is yours once the tank is full!!

Gas Refill

Cleaning Service

Standard Maintenance

Monthly Insurance

Tire Repacement

Emergency Reserve

Annual Fuel Budget

Audio System Upgrade

Initial Ownership Costs

Comprehensive Repair Fund

Vehicle Technology Enhancements

Purchase Down-payment

Write these fun details about your dream car

Car Model : ....

Color of your Car : ....

Date of Purchase : ....

Purchase Price : ....

Attach a picture of your dream car

Gaming and Electronics Fund

$60: A New Video Game for Their Console or PC

Video Games: A brand-new video game for a console or PC usually costs around $60. Teens might be saving for popular games on platforms like PlayStation, Xbox, Nintendo, or PC. With frequent game releases, keeping up with the latest titles can be expensive, making this a frequent savings goal for gamers.

In-Game Purchases: Some games also offer additional content like expansion packs or cosmetic upgrades, costing between $10 and $60, providing extra customization options and extending game enjoyment.

$200: Gaming Accessories

Headphones: High-quality gaming headphones, especially those with surround sound or noise-canceling features, typically cost between $100 and $200. These provide an immersive gaming experience and are a top choice for competitive gamers.

Controllers and Peripherals: Extra controllers for consoles, mechanical keyboards, or specialized gaming mice are other popular accessories, ranging from $50 to $150. Customizing a gaming setup with these tools enhances comfort and performance.

Streaming Gear: For teens interested in streaming, gear like webcams, microphones, and lighting equipment can cost anywhere from $100 to $200, helping them build a professional setup for content creation.

$400: PC Upgrade Components

Graphics Cards: One of the most important components for a gaming PC, a graphics card upgrade can drastically improve performance. These range from $200 to $400 for mid-range options. High-end cards can push prices even higher.

Monitors: Gamers often seek high-refresh-rate monitors or larger screens to elevate their gameplay experience. A solid gaming monitor typically costs $150 to $400, depending on size and features like resolution and response time.

$500+: Gaming Consoles and Major Upgrades

New Consoles: Gaming consoles like the PlayStation 5 or Xbox Series X cost around $500 or more, making them a significant savings goal for teens looking to upgrade to the latest system.

PC Builds/Upgrades: For PC gamers, building or significantly upgrading a gaming rig can easily exceed $500, particularly when factoring in high-end components like processors, motherboards, or additional storage.

Virtual Reality (VR) Sets: For teens interested in next-gen gaming, VR headsets like the Oculus or PlayStation VR range from $300 to $500, opening up an entirely new level of immersive gaming.

ELECTRONICS FUND

TARGET | MAX SAVED

SAVINGS GAME STARTS NOW!

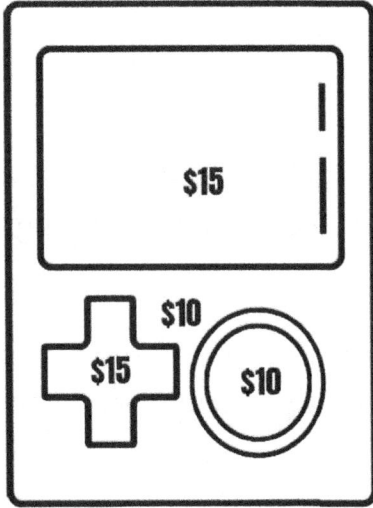

NEW VIDEO GAME – $60

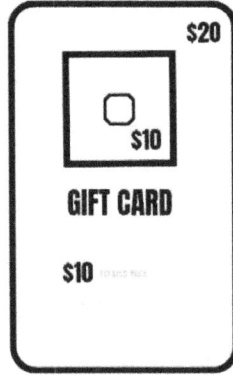

- $15
- $10
- $15
- $10

ACCESSORIES FOR GAMING – $100

- GIFT CARD: $20, $10, $10
- $20
- $10, $10, $10, $10

PC/LAPTOP UPGRAGE – $400

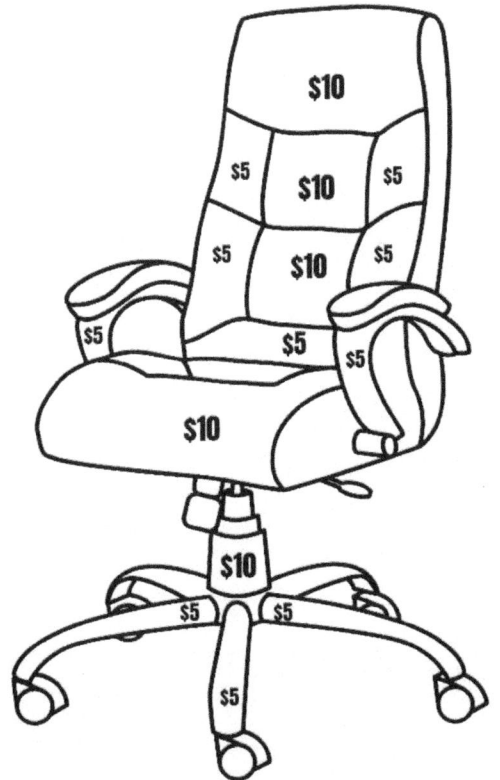

- UPDATED
- $200
- $50
- $25
- $25

Gaming chair:
- $10, $5, $10, $5, $5, $10, $5, $5, $5, $10, $10, $5, $5, $5

CONSOLE UPGRADE ($500+)

$250

$5

$25

$5

$25

$20

$20

$20

$25

$10

$20

$20

$25

$15

$15

$10

$10

GAMING & ELECTRONICS FUND LOG

New Video Game - $60		
%Saved	Amount Saved	Date
25%	$15	
50%	$30	
75%	$45	
100%	$60	

Accessories - $200		
%Saved	Amount Saved	Date
25%	$50	
50%	$100	
75%	$150	
100%	$200	

PC Upgrade - $400		
%Saved	Amount Saved	Date
25%	$100	
50%	$200	
75%	$300	
100%	$400	

New Gaming Console - $500+		
%Saved	Amount Saved	Date
25%	$125	
50%	$250	
75%	$375	
100%	$500	

Let's talk about gaming!!

Do you like gaming? : ....

Favorite Game : ....

High score you are proud of : ....

Any new game you want to play? : ....

Upgrade your electronics

PC/Laptop Model name & OS : ....

Is the software updated? : ....

Favorite Brand : ....

Does any device require upgrade/repair? : ....

Money Skills for Teens and Young Adults

Concerts and Music Festivals Fund

$50: Merchandise from Their Favorite Band or Artist

T-Shirts and Apparel: Concert t-shirts and hoodies often range from $20 to $50, depending on the band or event.

Posters and Memorabilia: Signed posters, albums, or limited-edition items are popular, usually priced between $20 and $50.

$50-$100: Ticket to a Local Concert or Small Music Festival

Local Concerts: Tickets to smaller shows typically cost $50 to $75, offering general admission to local performances.

Small Music Festivals: Day passes for small festivals are around $75 to $100, often featuring emerging artists.

General Admission: At this price range, tickets are usually general admission without VIP perks.

$200: Premium Tickets or Access to Larger Festivals

VIP or Premium Seating: Premium tickets with early entry or VIP perks can cost around $150 to $200.

Multi-Day Festival Access: A $200 budget could cover multi-day festival passes, offering access to multiple performances.

Meet-and-Greets: Some events offer special passes for meet-and-greets, which fall into the $150-$200 range.

$300-$500: Travel and Accommodation for Out-of-Town Festivals

Transportation: Travel to out-of-town festivals could range from $100 to $300, depending on distance.

Accommodation: Hotels or rentals near festival venues cost around $100-$200 per night, or opt for festival camping at $100-$300.

Spending Money: For food, drinks, and merchandise, budgeting $100-$200 is recommended.

Pro Tips for Festival-Goers

Group Savings: Splitting the cost of accommodation or carpooling with friends can cut down on expenses.

Early Bird Deals: Purchasing tickets early often saves money on both admission and travel.

Travel Hacks: Using loyalty points for flights or public transportation can help stretch savings for teens traveling out of town.

Concerts and Music Festivals Fund

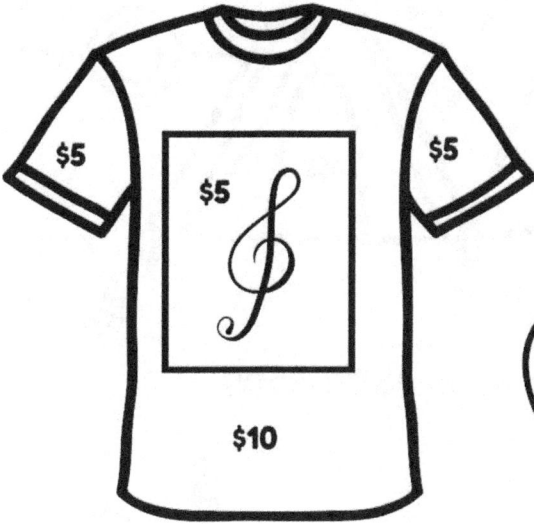

Goal

Saved

Merchandise - $25

$5

$5

$5

$10

Local concert - $50-$100

$10

$20

$20

$10

$20

TICKET

$10

$10

Premium Tickets - $200

$10

$10

$10 $10 $10

$10 $10

$10 $10

$10

$10

$20 $10

$20

BACKSTAGE PASS

$20

$20

$20

$10

$20

$20

$15

$15

$10

$15

$20

$15

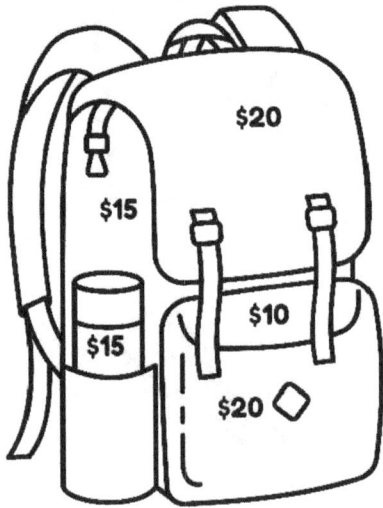

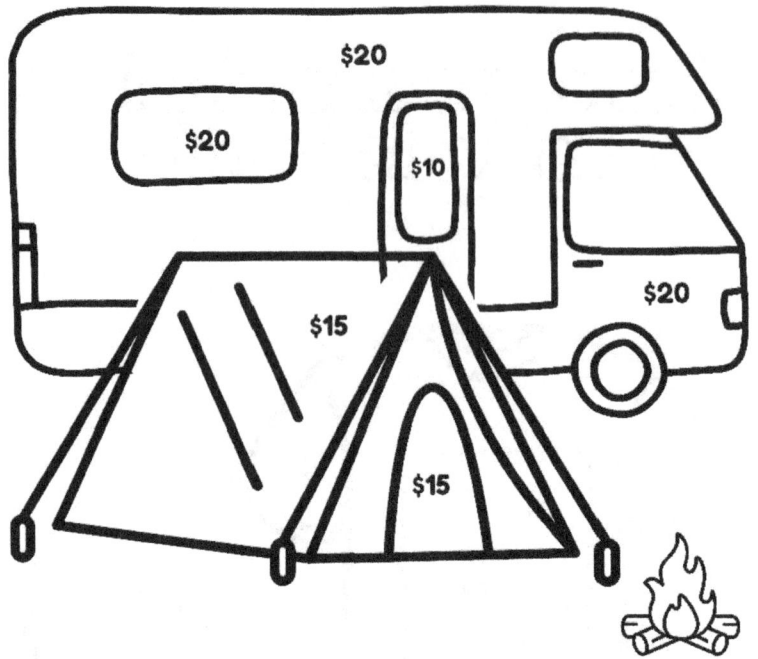

Concert/Event (out of town) - $300-$500

$15

$50

$15

$10

$10

$15

$20

$20

$10

$10

$20

$15

$10

Concerts & Music Festivals Fund Log

Color the notes whenever you complete the task

Merchandise ($25)		
%Saved	Amount Saved	Date
25%	$6.25	
50%	$12.5	
75%	$18.75	
100%	$25	

Local Concert ($50 - $100)		
%Saved	Amount Saved	Date
25%		
50%		
75%		
100%		

Premium Tickets for Concerts ($200)		
%Saved	Amount Saved	Date
25%	$50	
50%	$100	
75%	$150	
100%	$200	

Out-of-town Music Festival ($300-$500)		
%Saved	Amount Saved	Date
25%	$100	
50%	$200	
75%	$300	
100%	$400	

Write the lyrics you vibe with

Keep Calm • Listen to Music

Favorite Singer : ....

Favorite Band : ....

Favorite Song : ....

Dream Concert : ....

Attach a picture attending event/ Picture of your favorite singer(s)

Pet Savings Fund

Initial Purchase or Adoption Fee ($50–$300)

Adoption or Purchase: The cost of adopting or purchasing a pet can vary widely depending on the type of animal. Smaller pets like fish or reptiles typically cost around $50, while larger pets like dogs, cats, or exotic animals may range up to $300 or more.

Supplies ($100–$200)

Habitat Setup: For pets like birds or lizards, you'll need to set up a proper enclosure or tank, which can range from $50 to $150.

Bowls/Feeders: Essential items like feeding bowls or water dispensers can cost between $20 and $50, depending on the pet's needs.

Bedding/Toys: For pets like small mammals or reptiles, bedding or toys typically add an extra $20 to $50.

Grooming Tools: Basic tools such as brushes for furred animals or cleaning supplies for reptiles cost around $10 to $30.

Veterinary Care ($100–$500)

Check-Ups: Initial health screenings for your pet usually range from $100 to $300, depending on the animal. Exotic pets may require specialized care.

Spaying/Neutering: For dogs or cats, spaying or neutering services typically cost between $150 and $300.

Unexpected Visits: Emergency veterinary visits can cost up to $500 or more, depending on the situation.

Food ($20–$50/month)

Pet Food: Monthly food costs can range from $20 for smaller pets, like reptiles or hamsters, to $50 or more for larger animals such as dogs or cats.

Treats/Supplements: Additional treats or supplements can add $5 to $15 to your monthly pet expenses.

Training and Behavior ($50–$200)

Training: Pets like dogs or even some exotic pets may require behavioral training, costing between $50 and $150 per session, depending on the complexity of the training.

Grooming ($30–$100)

Home Grooming: Basic grooming tools for furred pets, like brushes or nail clippers, cost around $10 to $30.

Professional Grooming: Dogs or cats may need professional grooming services, which can range from $30 to $100 per session, depending on the size and breed of the pet.

Pet-Sitting or Boarding ($15–$50/day)

Boarding: When traveling, boarding your pet can range from $30 to $50 per day for dogs or cats. Smaller pets, such as lizards or birds, may cost between $15 and $30 per day.

Saving for Pet

Goal

Saved

Welcome the little friend without worrying about the expenses

Initial Purchase ($50-$300)

Pet Supplies ($100-$200)

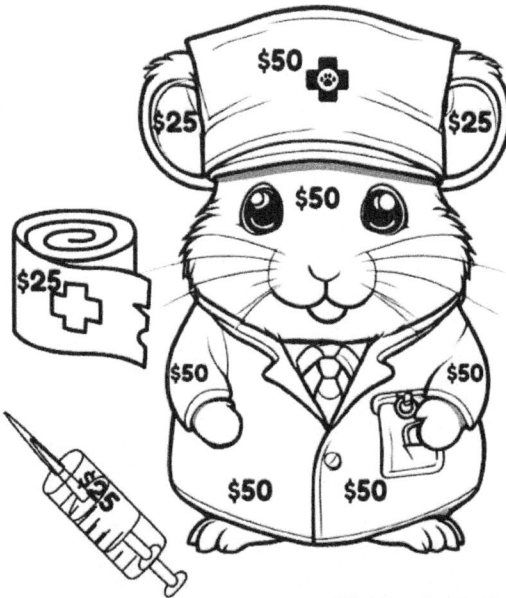

Veterinary care ($100-$500)

Food ($20-$50/month)

Money Skills for Teens and Young Adults

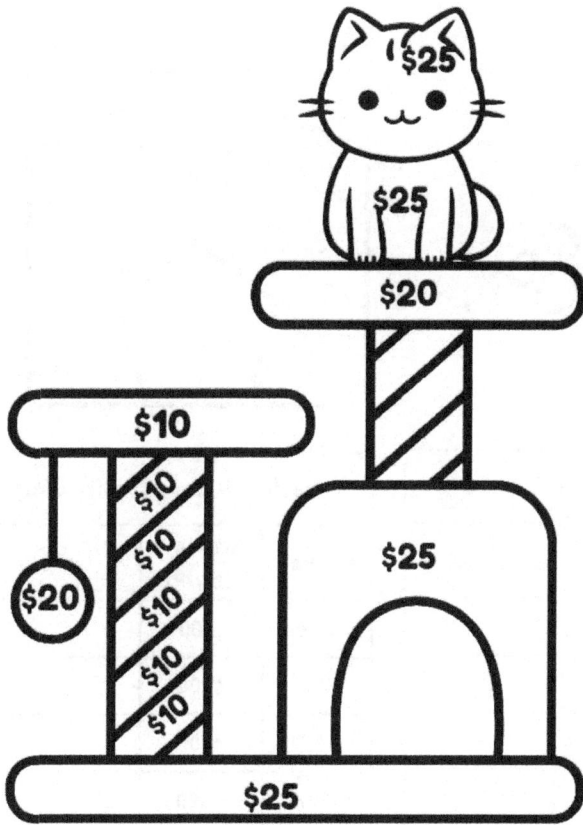

Training & Behavior ($50–$200)

Pet Grooming ($30–$100)

Pet sitting ($15–$50/day)

Miscellaneous ($10–$50)

Pet Savings Log

Write your pet's name after you finish coloring the house

Misc
Pet Sitting
Pet Grooming
Training & Behavior
Pet Food
Veterinary care
Pet Accessories
Initial Purchase

Initial Purchase ($50-$300)

%Saved	Amount Saved	Date
25%	$62.5	
50%	$125	
75%	$187.5	
100%	$250	

Pet Supplies ($100-$200)

%Saved	Amount Saved	Date
25%	$50	
50%	$100	
75%	$150	
100%	$200	

Veterinary Care ($100-$500)

%Saved	Amount Saved	Date
25%	$100	
50%	$200	
75%	$300	
100%	$400	

Food ($20-$50/month)

%Saved	Amount Saved	Date
25%	$12.5	
50%	$25	
75%	$37.5	
100%	$50	

Training & Behavior ($50-$200)

%Saved	Amount Saved	Date
25%	$50	
50%	$100	
75%	$150	
100%	$200	

Grooming ($30-$100)

%Saved	Amount Saved	Date
25%	$25	
50%	$50	
75%	$75	
100%	$100	

Pet Sitting ($15-$50/day)

%Saved	Amount Saved	Date
25%	$12.5	
50%	$25	
75%	$37.5	
100%	$50	

Miscellaneous ($10-$50)

%Saved	Amount Saved	Date
25%	$10	
50%	$20	
75%	$30	
100%	$40	

Take a picture of your pet and attach the photo here

Themed **Savings**

Using themed savings pages, like those for Valentine's Day, Mother's Day, or the holidays, helps you build a habit of being financially prepared, which can reduce a lot of last-minute stress. Setting aside small amounts over time means that when the holidays come, you'll already have enough to buy thoughtful gifts or plan something special without scrambling for money. This kind of planning teaches you how to manage your money for the things that matter now, but it's also setting you up for the future.

As an adult, being financially prepared can make a big difference when it comes to larger expenses like home improvements, vacations, or even emergencies. Just like saving for a holiday gift, saving ahead for a home project means you won't be caught off guard by costs, and you can enjoy the results without worrying about how you'll pay for them. Planning ahead for vacations means less stress leading up to your trip and more enjoyment once you're there. The skill of setting a savings goal and sticking to it now will help you handle bigger responsibilities later in life, making things like buying a car, starting a family, or even just enjoying life's little moments a lot less stressful.

HAPPY Valentines DAY

WHY JUST WISH
WHEN YOU CAN GIFT!!

TARGET

SAVED

Money Skills for Teens and Young Adults

Spring BREAK

BUDGET

SAVED

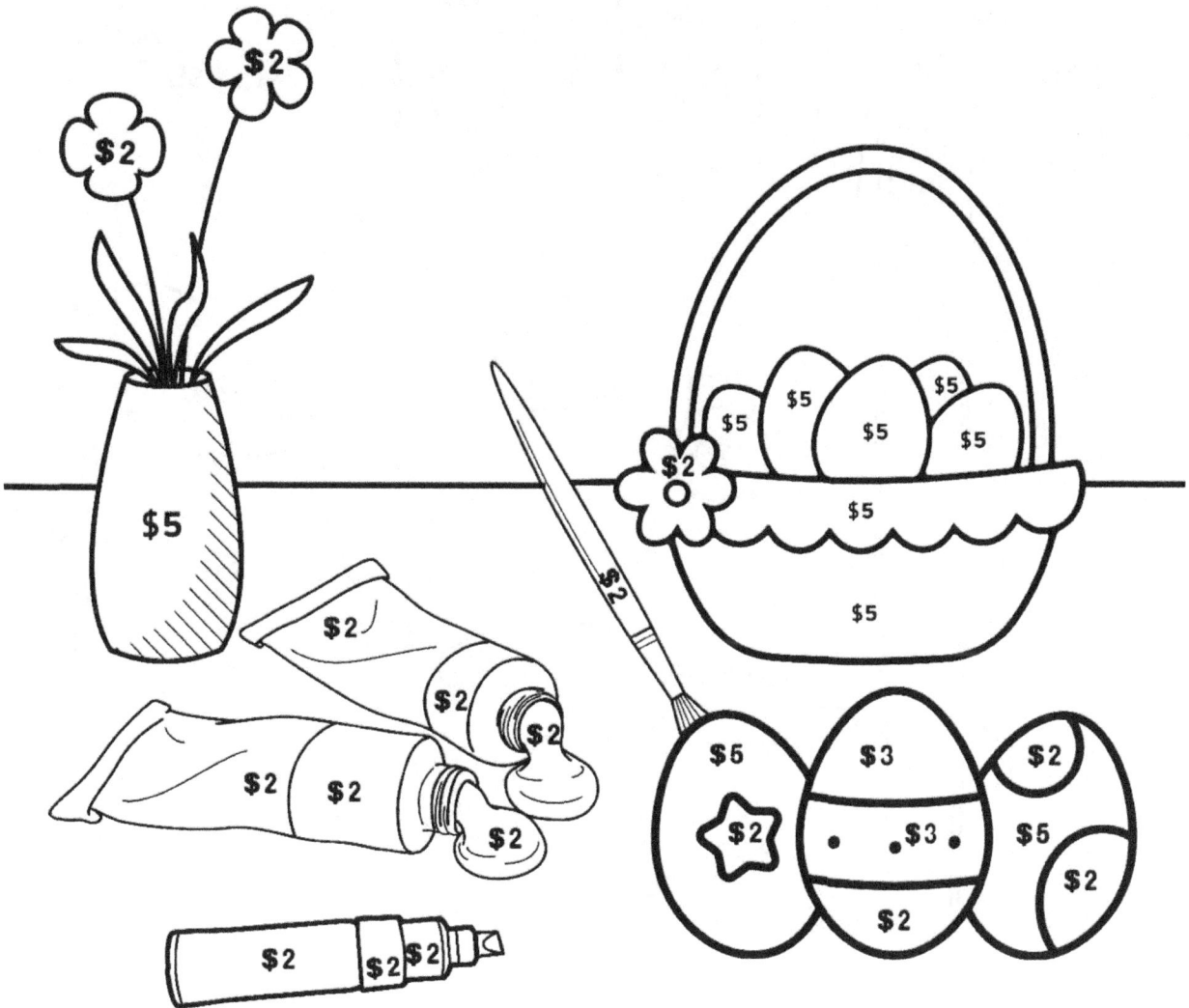

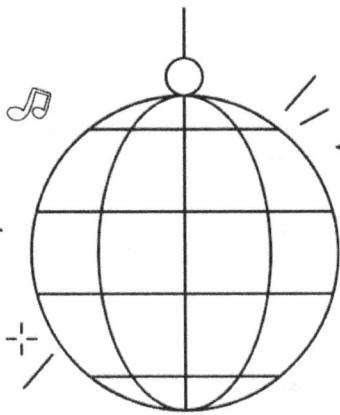

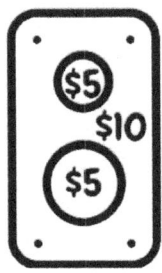
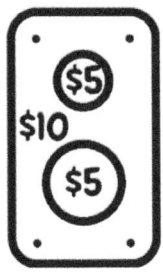

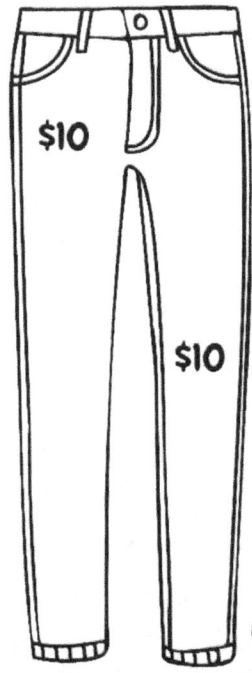

Money Skills for Teens and Young Adults

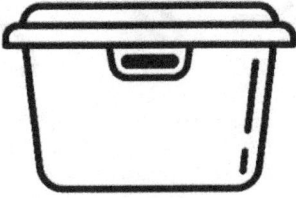

BUDGET

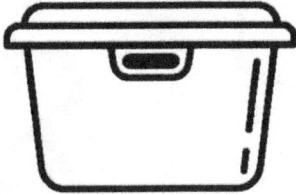

SAVED

HAPPY

Mother's

DAY

$5

$10

$5
$5
$5
$5

$15

$10

$5 $5

$5

$10 $5 $10

$10 $10 $10

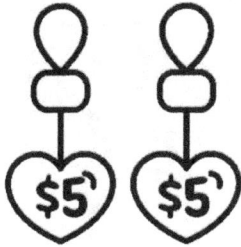

$10 $5

Mom

BUDGET

SAVED

$15 $5 $15

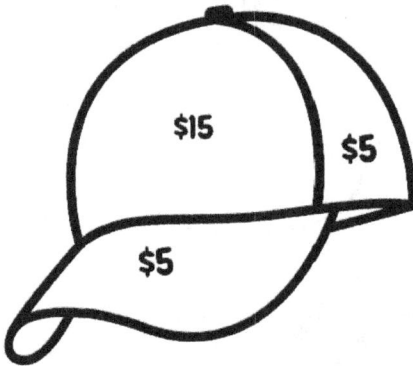

$15 $5
$5

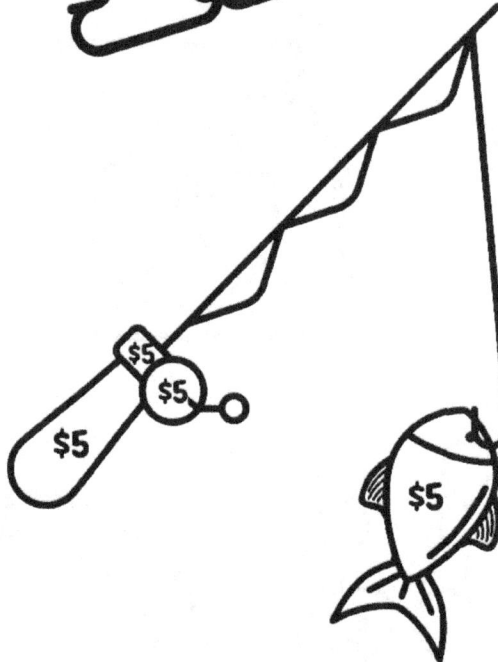

$5 $5
$5
$5

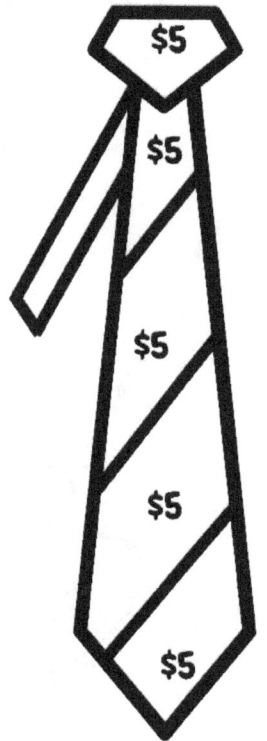

$5
$5
$5
$5
$5

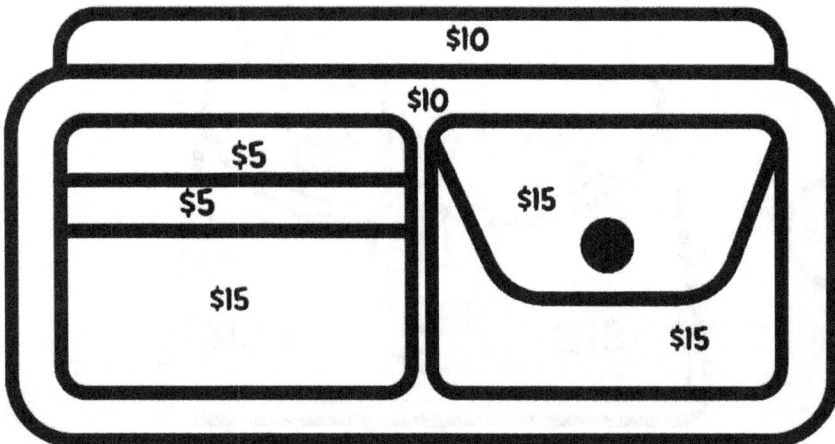

$10
$10
$5
$5
$15
$15
$15

$10
$5
$5

Summer
BREAK

BUDGET

SAVED

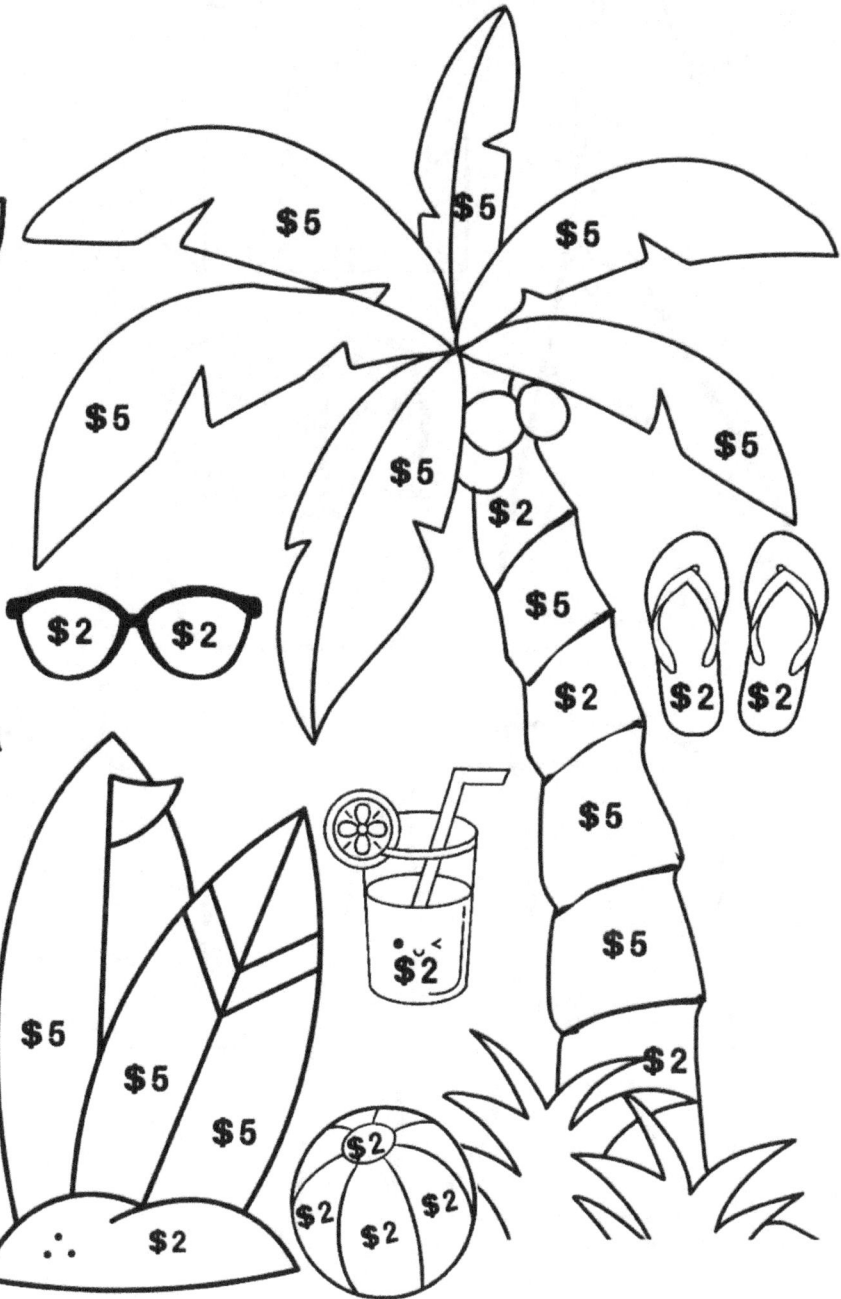

HAPPY BIRTHDAY

$1 $1 $1 $1 $1 $1 $1 $1 $1

Budget   Saved

$5 $5
$10

$1
$10 $5

$5
$10

$5 $5 $5

$5

HBD
$5

$5 $5

$5
$1
$1 $1
$5
$5
$1 $1
$5
$1 $5 $1
$1 $1
$5
$5
$5

BUDGET   SAVED

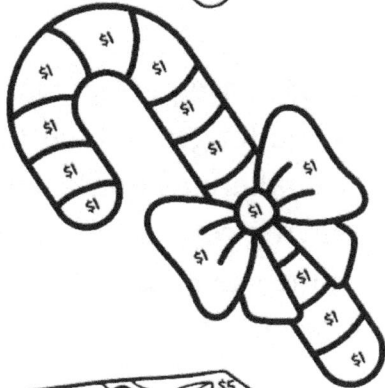

Flexible Dollar Challenges

Dollar challenges, like the $50, $100, or $500 challenges, are perfect warm-ups for building your savings. Unlike themed savings challenges, which focus on specific goals like holidays or events, these dollar challenges don't have a set purpose—they're more about getting you in the habit of saving consistently. The idea is to get comfortable setting aside smaller amounts of money regularly, helping you develop discipline without feeling overwhelmed by a big target.

These challenges are great for getting started, especially if you're not sure what you want to save for yet. Completing a $50 or $100 challenge is a small win, but it builds momentum. The best part is, you'll have extra cash set aside for whatever comes up in the future. Maybe it's something fun, or maybe it's something practical, but either way, you'll be ready. These smaller challenges help you form good habits that will make saving for larger goals easier down the road, whether that's for bigger savings challenges or just having a little financial cushion when you need it.

$50 SAVINGS CHALLENGE

Color the stars as you save.
They shine just as bright as you

$50 SAVINGS CHALLENGE

You got this!

Complete coloring the beautiful clouds as you save

$5

$2 $2

$5 $3 $5

$3 $3

$2 $2 $2

$3 $3

$5 $3 $5

$2 $2

$5

$50 SAVINGS CHALLENGE

Color the stars as you save.
They shine just as bright as you

$5 $4 $2

$5 $3 $5 $3

$4 $3 $2

$5 $3 $5 $2

$4 $2 $5

$50 SAVINGS CHALLENGE

**Complete coloring
the beautiful clouds
as you save**

$5

$2 $2

$5 $3 $5

$3 $3

$2 $2 $2

$3 $3

$5 $3 $5

$2 $2

$5

    Money Skills for Teens and Young Adults

$100 SAVINGS CHALLENGE

Savings so bright that the Sunflower follows.

$100 Savings Challenge

Countdown for the savings start 3,2,1... Save!!

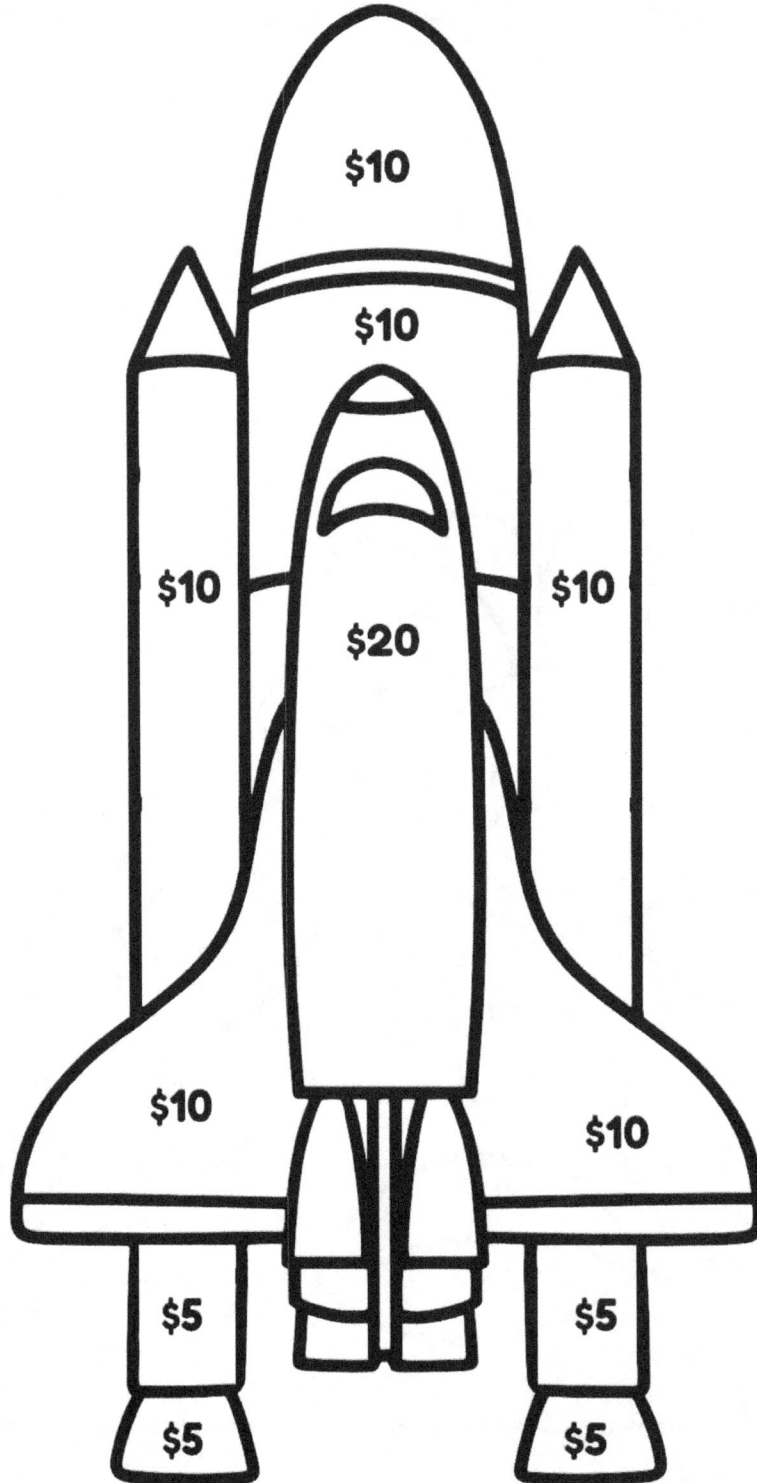

$10

$10

$10

$10

$20

$10

$10

$5

$5

$5

$5

Money Skills for Teens and Young Adults

$100 SAVINGS CHALLENGE

Savings so bright that the sunflower follows.

$100 Savings Challenge

Countdown for the savings start 3,2,1... Save!!

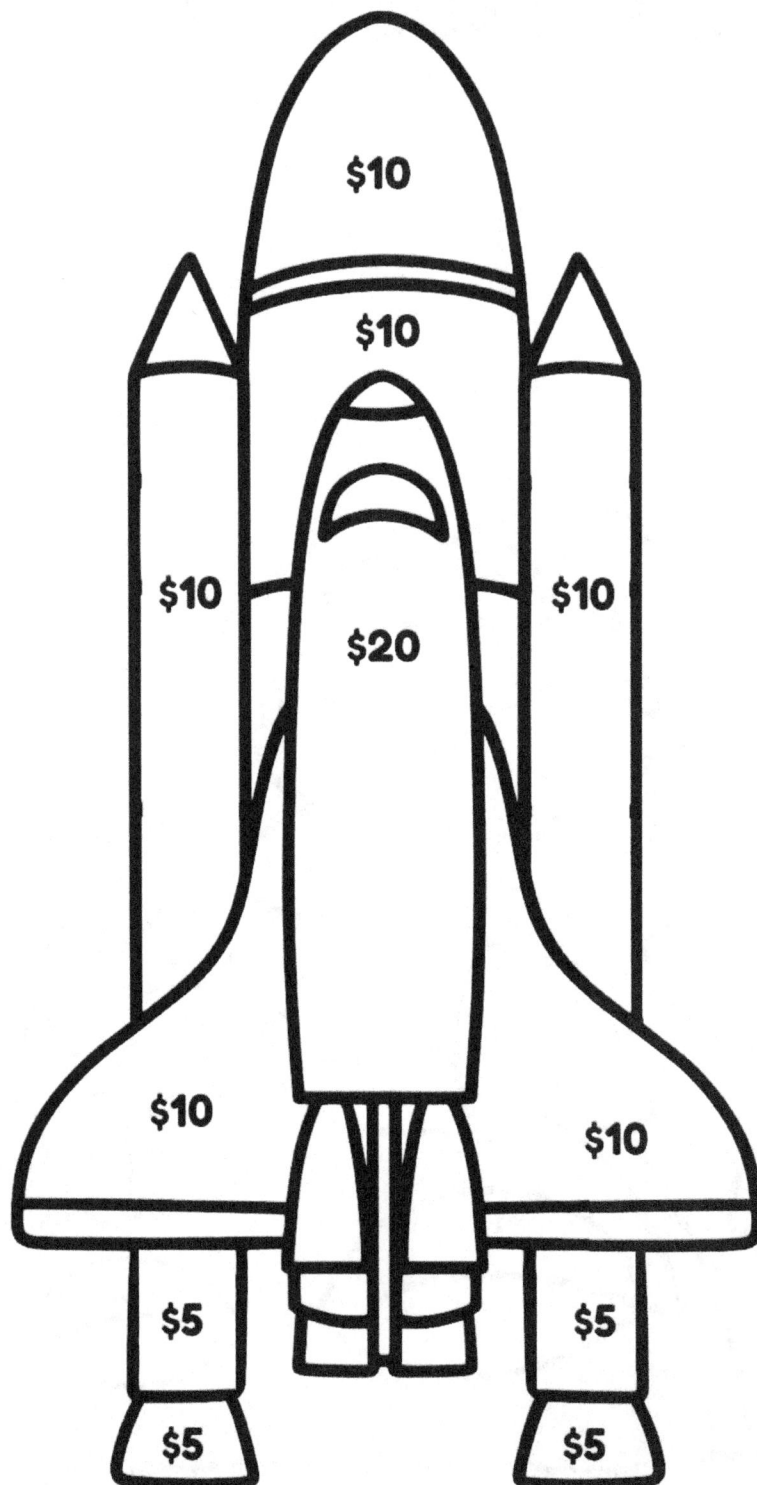

$10

$10

$10

$10

$20

$10

$10

$5

$5

$5

$5

Money Skills for Teens and Young Adults

$500 Savings challenge!!

Purpose _____   Status _____

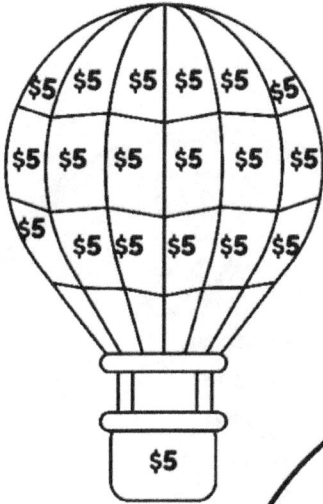

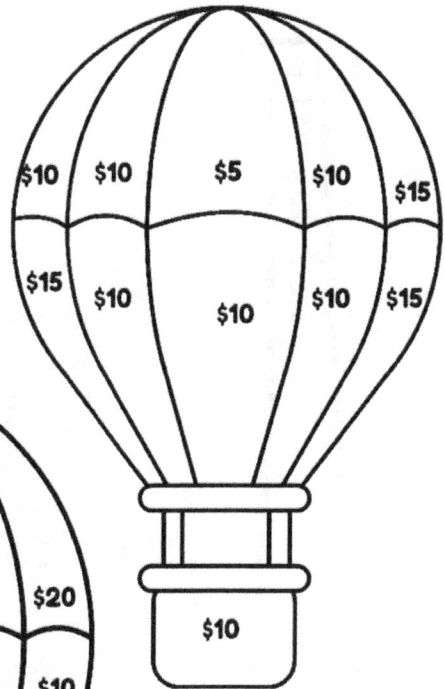

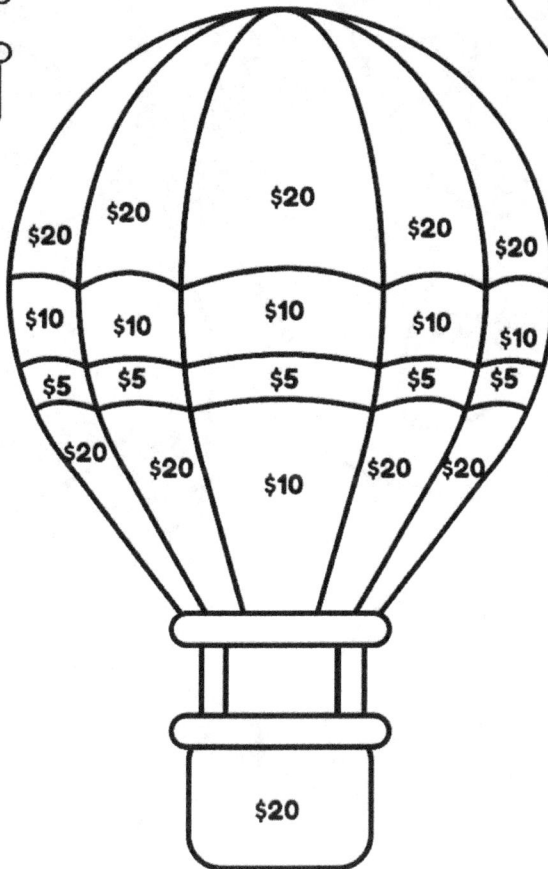

$500 Savings Challenge

Hit a Home-run in savings!!

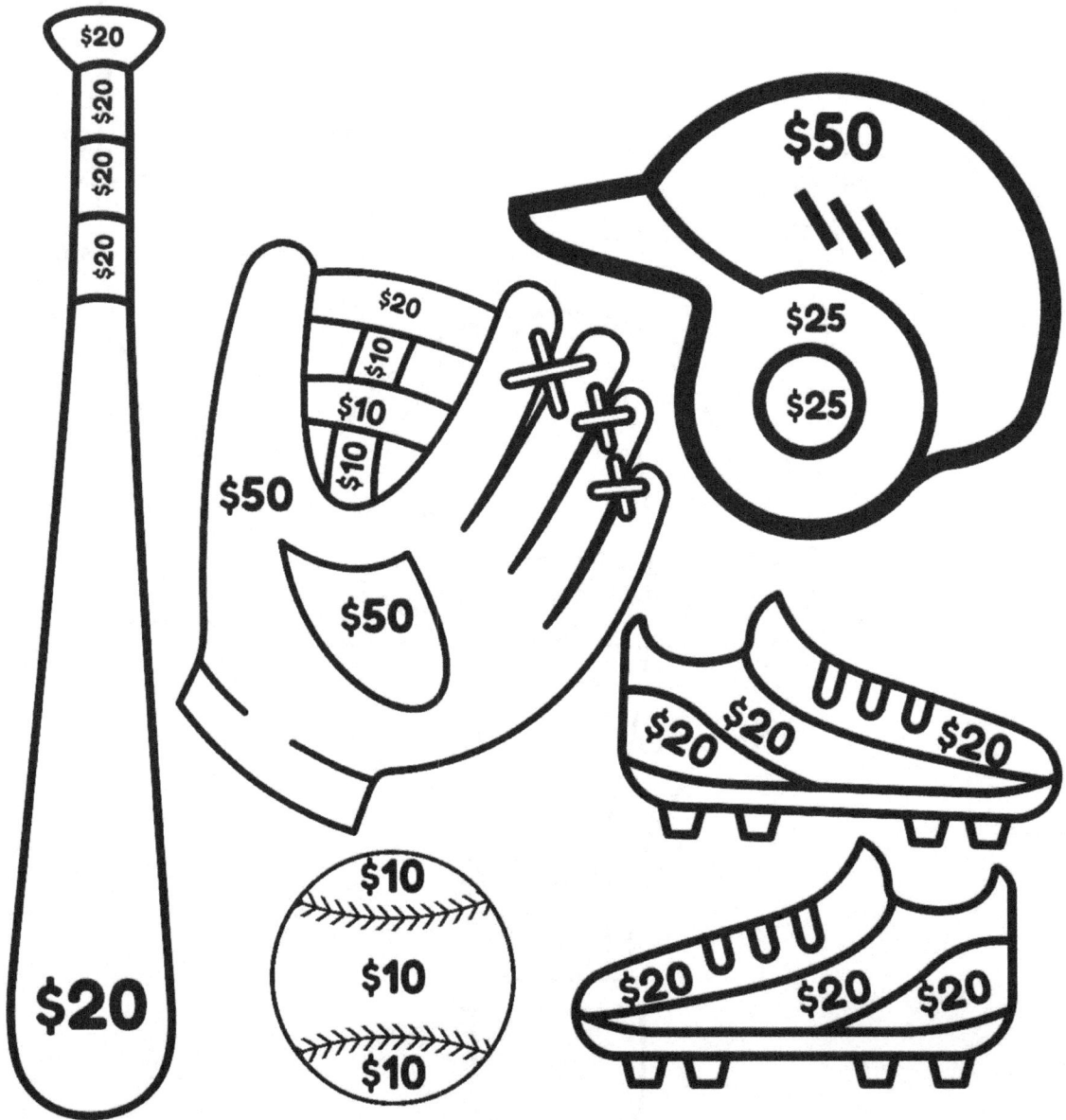

Money Skills for Teens and Young Adults

BONUS:
Additional Savings Trackers

Name of the challenge

....

Follow the example to keep a log of your cash savings & spendings

- When You Saved $15
- When You Saved $5
- When You Spent $10

Example

DATE	AMOUNT	TOTAL
10/10/2024	$15	$15
10/11/2024	$5	$20
10/12/2024	-$10	$10

Add / Subtract

DATE	AMOUNT	TOTAL

DATE	AMOUNT	TOTAL

Money Skills for Teens and Young Adults

Name of the challenge

....

Follow the example to keep a log of your cash savings & spendings

- When You Saved $15
- When You Saved $5
- When You Spent $10

Example

DATE	AMOUNT	TOTAL
10/10/2024	$15	$15
10/11/2024	$5	$20
10/12/2024	-$10	$10

Add
Subtract

DATE	AMOUNT	TOTAL

DATE	AMOUNT	TOTAL

Name of the challenge

....

Follow the example to keep a log of your cash savings & spendings

👉

- When You Saved $15
- When You Saved $5
- When You Spent $10

Example

DATE	AMOUNT	TOTAL
10/10/2024	$15	$15
10/11/2024	$5	$20
10/12/2024	-$10	$10

Add
Subtract

DATE	AMOUNT	TOTAL

DATE	AMOUNT	TOTAL

DIGITAL SAVINGS TRACKER

CHECK BOOK

NAME OF THE
DEPOSITOR: ....

SAVING FOR: ....

Keep a track of all your Digital Savings

DEPOSIT DATE	DIGITAL SOURCE	AMOUNT DEPOSITED (+)	AMOUNT SPENT (-)	NET SAVINGS

DIGITAL SAVINGS TRACKER

CHECK BOOK

NAME OF THE
DEPOSITOR: ....

SAVING FOR: ....

Keep a track of all your Digital Savings

DEPOSIT DATE	DIGITAL SOURCE	AMOUNT DEPOSITED (+)	AMOUNT SPENT (-)	NET SAVINGS

Money Skills for Teens and Young Adults

DIGITAL SAVINGS TRACKER

CHECK BOOK

NAME OF THE
DEPOSITOR: ....

SAVING FOR: ....

Keep a track of all your Digital Savings

DEPOSIT DATE	DIGITAL SOURCE	AMOUNT DEPOSITED (+)	AMOUNT SPENT (-)	NET SAVINGS

DOUBLE BONUS CONTENT!

Feel free to print these pages for your personal use as you work through the challenges in this book. However, please remember that these materials are copyrighted and are meant just for you. Sharing them with others, either digitally or in print, would be considered a violation of copyright. Let's respect the hard work that went into creating them by keeping them for your personal use only.

Thank you for understanding, and enjoy putting these tools to good use! Scan below to find the extra pages

Made in the USA
Coppell, TX
17 July 2025

52046621R00072